INDIGENOUS PEOPLES

A Fieldguide for Development

Development Guidelines, No.2.
(Series Editor: Brian Pratt)

John Beauclerk and Jeremy Narby
with Janet Townsend

Published May 1988
© Oxfam 1988

British Library Cataloguing in Publication Data

Beauclerk, John
   Indigenous peoples: a fieldguide
   for development.
   1. Developing countries. Development
   projects. Administration
   I. Title. II. Narby, Jeremy
   III. Townsend, Janet
   338.9'009172'4

   ISBN 0-85598-087-0
   ISBN 0-85598-088-5 Pbk

Published by Oxfam, 274 Banbury Road, Oxford OX2 7DZ, UK.
Typeset by Typo Graphics, Oxford
Printed by Oxfam Print Unit

Contents

PART TWO   ADVICE

Section 1   APPROPRIATE ACTIVITIES FOR NON-GOVERNMENTAL ORGANISATIONS

Section 2   FIELD METHODS

Preface

Throughout the world there are minority peoples who lead their lives independently of the nation state. Over generations they have watched national boundaries harden around and through their territories until they have become outcasts in their own lands. Economic growth has further undermined these people by encroaching on their land base and transforming the environments on which they depend for their survival.

This manual is for fieldworkers in NGOs (non-governmental organisations) who work with indigenous peoples. It presents some ways in which indigenous peoples can reverse the general trend and cope with change. In writing it, we began with the experience of the indigenous peoples of western Amazonia. With the support of NGOs over the last twenty years, many indigenous groups of this area have taken steps to defend their lands from invasion. They have devised a model of change that builds on their traditional self-reliance and strengthens their negotiating position with the state. This manual shows how this and other models offer hope to other indigenous peoples.

The book is divided into two parts. The first examines experience, the second presents advice. Part One, Experience, describes the main features of indigenous societies and reviews the different ways in which governments and other institutions have sought to change them (Section 1). Unfortunately most interventions planned to affect indigenous lives have been highly damaging (Section 2), but the conditions found to be necessary for indigenous self-management are also recorded (Section 3). Part Two, Advice, sets out with some practical detail activities in which NGOs have been of use to indigenous people (Section 1). Part Two concludes with specific advice to NGO representatives in the field, guiding them through some of the many pitfalls they are likely to encounter (Section 2).

Acknowledgements are due to: Frederica Barclay, Jo Boyden, Alberto Chirif, Shelton H. Davis, Steve Duke, Pedro Garcia, Carolyn Heath, John Hemming, Christine Hugh-Jones, Soren Hvalkof, Robert Layton, Kathe Mentzen, Thomas Moore, Evaristo Nugkuag, Hope Page, Brian Pratt, Renato Rosaldo, Richard Smith, Charles and Jan Staver, Sally Swenson, Lucy Trapnell, David Turton, Stefano Varese, Hanne Veber, Lissie Wahl, Patricio and Angela Warren, Christine Whitehead.

We also thank the Amazonian people with whom we lived for showing us the importance of listening. To them we dedicate this book in the hope that it can in some way repay them for their patience.

Special thanks also to:-

The Leverhulme Trust, for financial support during the research and writing; Survival International, for support and advice.

PART ONE:
EXPERIENCE

INDIGENOUS PEOPLES

I. Introduction

In every continent there are human groups whose ethnic characteristics, cultural traditions and methods of using resources and technology distinguish them from the majority of people in the nation state. Even though their culture, social organisation and economy vary greatly from one group to another, and between groups even within the same country, the indigenous groups that have survived today are all vulnerable to discrimination, exploitation and oppression and, in extreme circumstances, exposure to physical or cultural extinction. It is these features of indigenous people — their separateness in ethnic terms and their uncertain relations with the national society — that put them so much at risk.

II. Characteristic features

There are roughly 200 million indigenous people in the world, approximately 4 per cent of the total population. They live in extremely varied environments, generally harsh and remote, such as tundras, drylands and rainforests, from which they satisfy all their needs. Their mode of subsistence is as varied as their environments: they may practise fishing, hunting, gathering, pastoral nomadism, cultivation, or a range of these in combination. Economic activities are a part of traditional life and are controlled through social institutions such as marriage, kinship, age groups, clans and public rituals. Traditional societies gain great strength from the integration of economic, social, religious and political affairs.

Many indigenous people can no longer meet their subsistence needs from their own resources, and engage in other income-generating activities. All too often, this means casual wage labour, often migrant, contracted on very unfavourable terms. They may accept this as the only way of keeping their culture alive and there is obviously a shading from truly subsistence indigenous societies to those with a substantial engagement with the national economy.

Despite the variety among indigenous peoples around the world, some generalisations may usefully be made.

1. Sustainable use of resources

The economies of all indigenous peoples are closely adapted to their natural resources of which they reveal a high degree of knowledge based on observation and long practice. A particular feature of the technologies developed by indigenous peoples for subsistence is their emphasis on the sustainable use of their resources. Indigenous peoples practising traditional subsistence are somewhere near an ecological balance with their surroundings; a group which was not so would be short lived. This balance does not mean that indigenous peoples do not exploit and manage the environment, but there is a stability underlying this management in most cases. Mobility is often a key factor. Forest dwellers, for instance, operate long-term rotations for their gardens and allow game to restock by moving their settlements regularly. Pastoral nomads often have intricate schedules which allow them to take advantage of irregular supplies of water and grazing.

2. Land held in common

Indigenous peoples are entitled to rights of occupation of their lands which should be recognised by national society. They generally regard ownership of land as communal, vested in all the members of a particular group, or perhaps of a clan or subgroup. Traditionally, purchase plays no part in rights to land. The resource-holding group may own a territory, or a group of religious sites, or a water hole; in rare cases there may be no group asserting ownership of resources. Access to the group may be by inheritance, or by place of birth, or by admission by the group. The relationship of the people to their territories is rarely just economic; normally it is closely identified with their spiritual beliefs. Peoples such as the Aborigines of Australia, who have been dispossessed of much of their lands, will still do all in their power to protect ceremonial sites and natural features of ritual significance.

Pastoral groups may share land or water with other groups, often using it at different times but still depending on it for survival; their rights may be of access to water rather than land. By their very nature, many rangelands and forest reserves have no physical marks identifying them, and may thus be labelled "unoccupied" by the state.

Foragers, or hunter-gatherers, are the extreme case. The means of production are collectively owned: everyone has access to the making of tools, and rights of reciprocal access to the resources of others are common.

3. Wealth shared equally

The economies of indigenous peoples are also comparatively undifferentiated, with the principal divisions of labour established on lines of gender and age. The minimum production unit is an essentially self-sufficient group of families. Within the indigenous economy there is often little opportunity for individual accumulation of wealth; people tend to maintain social cohesion by encouraging generosity. Indeed there are frequently social mechanisms that govern the redistribution of wealth within the group. Generosity may be an adaptation to sporadic supply, or may be an independent ethos, but equitable sharing is a common outcome.

These are not societies without problems, but the problems derive their particular character from their relations of production. For instance, foraging peoples usually value sharing, reciprocity, hard work and even temper; individuals who wish to hoard, to be lazy, to dominate others, to isolate themselves or be quick to argue and fight face ridicule, misfortune and social isolation.

4. Societies rooted in kinship

Every indigenous group has a distinct way of organising its own society and there are always collective structures governing the behaviour of individuals in every aspect of life. The organisation of the !Kung San of the Kalahari appears flexible, but is still the product of specific principles. Ritual plays an important role in social relations and the cohesion of peoples within indigenous societies is often maintained by a web of kinship that can spread out from, say, a nuclear family to include all members of the group; the !Kung San now use kinship ties to enable individuals to move between hunter/gatherer, pastoral and agricultural livelihoods.

The strength of indigenous peoples ultimately rests on the kinship groups and the way these groups individually or collectively conduct their political, economic and religious affairs. Among most indigenous peoples, groups enjoy considerable local autonomy in the exercise of authority and only a shared threat will bring a large number of groups together for a common enterprise such as defence of land. Kinship structures provide individuals with security and give them an established role within the group as a whole. A common language, culture and system of religious beliefs may reinforce identification of the individual within the group.

On the other hand, conflicts between and within groups may exist and in some cases may be resolved by violence. Many of these rivalries and antagonisms are ritualised and limited by tradition, though outside influences may disrupt this.

5. Vulnerability

The very characteristics that have equipped indigenous peoples to survive in harsh environments and develop viable and satisfying social and economic systems can make them vulnerable when contacts are made with members of national societies. Most countries with indigenous populations within their boundaries have highly centralised political, legal and economic systems with complex division of labour. Without cultural adjustment, indigenous peoples cannot express their collective interests at national level. Kinship and reciprocity can easily break down when monetary relations are established. Traditional land ownership is no defence against the concept of private property. Population densities may be relatively low, livelihoods may be based on mobility and no taxable surplus may be produced: governments may see these as justification for dispossessing indigenous peoples. Ecologically sound subsistence systems are not regarded as a benefit to the country, but rather as a waste of resources. Indigenous peoples who seek to defend their territories and their autonomy find it difficult to adapt sufficiently without losing their identity.

III. The present situation of indigenous peoples

Many of the minority ethnic groups that have survived as distinct entities into the 20th century inhabit remote lands which formerly had no value for others. But material aspirations and technical advance have driven states to exploit resources previously regarded as marginal and uneconomic. The search for exports, the expanding populations, the spread of modern communications, the discovery of minerals and oil and the need to establish the frontiers of the nation state have reduced the isolation of many groups. Indigenous groups now face many pressures. They find their lands threatened by agriculture, irrigation projects, dams, highways, hydro-electric facilities, mines, agribusiness and timber extraction. These activities are often associated with national development projects in which indigenous people and their welfare are not a high priority. Even when the original population of an area identified for "development" is taken into account, the pace of environmental transformation is often so rapid that no allowance is made for adjustment to the new conditions. This alone may cause many indigenous peoples to oppose change designed for and by others. Indigenous peoples' resources are often appropriated without compensation. Their reluctance to sacrifice lands and culture to projects from which they will not benefit exposes them to further pressure. This is frequently manifested in national prejudices which may find expression in repressive legal codes. In extreme cases the incorporation of indigenous people into national society is still accompanied by violence, amounting on occasions to systematic physical abuse. This can happen even when indigenous groups have not resorted to violence themselves. Even where the law is to some extent favourable to indigenous peoples, its application is often at fault. When strong national interests oppose those of ethnic

6

minorities, as in most disputes over land and water, the laws protecting the weaker ethnic group are often flouted by the powerful.

It is in rich, industrialised countries that there have recently been different outcomes. Court decisions in Canada and Australia have gone in favour of indigenous peoples despite the efforts of the powerful business interests arrayed against them. The Dene of Canada's Northwest Territories seem to have fought big business to a standstill for the present; in the Northern Territory of Australia, the Aborigines can veto mineral prospecting on their land. Along with this has come a resurgence of traditional subsistence activities: some Aboriginal groups in central Australia, and the James Bay Cree in Canada, are doing more foraging today than ten years ago. Back to the land movements are favoured by governments; Canada has found it much cheaper to service a family at a trapping camp than to keep them on welfare at the main settlement, while the resurgence of hunting and gathering in Australia has reduced the number of Aborigines on welfare payments. There are risks of containment policies here, but the struggle for valuable lands is a positive one with significance for indigenous peoples around the world.

In poor countries, where essential services such as education and health are generally inadequate, low-status indigenous groups are often denied access to these services altogether, especially if their labour is not essential to the national economy. Those who do receive some basic provision frequently find it inappropriate to their society and culture. Official education programmes, for instance, may be used by governments as a tool for assimilation, to displace indigenous languages and cultures and to promote the national culture. Children may still be taken forcibly from their parents in the name of education.

IV. Enforced isolation

1. The case in favour
Some argue that contact with traditional groups, including "development work" by anthropologists, should be discouraged altogether because it is bound to undermine and ultimately to destroy traditional values and ways of life. Any change in closed indigenous societies may set in motion a sequence of transformations that will inevitably have a destructive effect on every aspect of the people's lives. To avoid this, some advocate the enforced isolation of these groups.

The "isolationist" view has arisen because often interventions intended to benefit indigenous peoples have actually caused harm, leading to deterioration in livelihood and an undermining of the group's concept of

7

itself and the relations of the members to each other and to the environment. Indigenous people have the right to refuse contact.

2. The case against

Official programmes with this "human zoo" approach are rare but do occur. In the Philippines, the Tasaday were protected by armed guards and a worldwide publicity campaign — protected mainly, perhaps, for their scientific interest. Isolationism also occurs in countries where conservation is strongly related to tourist industries. Botswana has the highest ratio per head of land in reserves of any country in the world. The Central Kalahari Game Reserve was originally established to protect traditionally foraging San populations and the flora and fauna upon which they depend. Now between a quarter and a half of the population leaves in the dry season for paid work, while, in the Reserve, San may be arrested for hunting.

The Manu National Park in southern Peru is an example of the way in which protection of the flora and fauna of a region can prejudice the original inhabitants, forcing them into a dependent position with no choice over cultural change. The Manu National Park covers one and a half million hectares. Five indigenous groups with an unknown total population occupy the conservation area. Even before the Park had achieved legal status in 1973 a dispute arose between its promoters and protestant missionaries over the status of a Machiguenga settlement at Tayakome, within the proposed boundaries. Park rules prohibit the use of firearms and the practice of market agriculture in any form and even discourage the use by indigenous people of trade goods. Half the families at Tayakome decided to follow the missionaries to a new site so that they could be incorporated into the market economy on their own terms. This community is now reported to be flourishing around a school and is in possession of title deeds to 9,000 hectares of land. Those Machiguenga remaining in Manu National Park have retained much of their traditional lifestyle as prescribed, but their future well-being is directly tied to the will of the Park authorities and to the fate of the Park. This is threatened by highway projects, by invasions of impoverished peasants from the Andes and by oil companies which are now applying for concessions in the Park. The result will depend on the degree of Peru's commitment to indigenous land rights.

The enforced isolation strategy has four principal defects:

i. Difficulty. Since penetration of indigenous territories is frequently prior to any establishment of land rights, "human zoo" policies can be unenforceable. The Brazilian government passed repeated decrees forbidding non-Indian access to the mineral-rich lands of the Yanomami, but tens of thousands of miners successfully disobeyed them.

ii. Loss of rights. It can effectively deprive indigenous peoples of the right to make their own decisions.

iii. Denial of skills. It can deprive them of the skills and knowledge required to defend themselves. The Cuna of Panama have successfully declared a large tract of their traditional territory to be a fauna reserve, accessible only to themselves and to scientists whom they approve. Their success is founded on years of contact and self-organisation.

iv. Paternalism. Isolation is invariably a harmful strategy when it is imposed by outsiders who take it upon themselves to interpret the needs of an indigenous group. It can become a means of controlling the relations that indigenous people themselves seek, restricting all contacts to one channel. This may occasionally be necessary in very extreme conditions (for example, people exposed to imported disease for the first time), but in the long run the groups themselves must make the contacts that they desire and feel they need. In the Kakadu National Park in Australia, aboriginal land management is part of Park policy; in Canada, the Dene have achieved the right to participate in wildlife management. Conversely, some Amazonian groups have sought to opt for isolation. Where that is their decision, it is their right.

Most indigenous groups in the world already find their traditional lifestyles considerably altered by contact with others. Enforced isolation would prevent them from meeting their present situation by acquiring new knowledge and skills to add to what remains of their own. It would be ideal if indigenous people could be left alone forever and not have to face the disruptive effect of the outside world. This can only be achieved where their land rights are truly respected. Where land rights are effectively as well as constitutionally guaranteed, indigenous peoples can exercise their right to refuse contact if they wish.

In too many cases, contact with the military, with highway builders, oil men, miners, travelling traders, settlers or missionaries is inevitable. Indigenous people will then need to acquire for themselves such defensive skills as knowledge of the national language, literacy, numeracy and where necessary, more advanced training in administration and accountancy. In the 1960s, it was suggested that the Gran Pajonal of the central Peruvian jungle be sealed off to protect the Ashaninca. Since there was already enough contact seriously to prejudice traditional life, the Ashaninca began rather to seek self-management based on land title, and they have indeed gained a measure of independence from the incoming settlers.

Anthropologists who seek to isolate groups from change may be felt to have more regard for the traditional culture than for the people. Extreme positions restricting the access of indigenous groups to change are often rooted in feeling that it will undermine cultural elements that are essential to the group's well-being. Even though sincerely held, this argument may lead to making a fetish of traditional culture — to treating it as a museum object or an endangered species. Cultures cannot "suffer" — people can. All societies, even the most remote, are continually changing, and those who live in indigenous societies are usually only too well aware of ways in which their lives could be improved. Respect must be shown for traditional culture because people need it; it is all they have to work with to make sense of their new situation. It is the people who are important.

v. Conclusion. The question for both fieldworkers and indigenous groups facing change is how to exploit the useful features of modern society without alienation and suffering. There are no ready made formulae to solve this problem; it confronts every indigenous people today, it arises in every programme set up by them or on their behalf, and it must be resolved according to the individual situation.

V. The future

Some groups may choose total integration with national society, on the grounds that it is the most effective way of surviving. However, integration schemes mounted by governments are more often than not thinly disguised attempts to draw indigenous people into the national economy as cheap labour. Other groups, such as those of western Amazonia, have sought the guarantee of fundamental human rights and equality of access to services through self-determination, or co-existence, rather than integration. Groups in Canada and Australia are engaged in similar strategies. In all these cases, autonomous political organisations have been formed to represent their people, lobby for more humane and appropriate government policies, and control and administer new programmes. National and international solidarity movements have grown alongside, and have helped to oppose the worst abuses.

International and national lobbying has reduced but not eliminated the most extreme violations of the human rights of indigenous peoples. There are also limitations to lobbying when governments use an ideology of national autonomy to justify policies of integration. The economic recession throughout the world has intensified pressure for the unplanned, short-term exploitation of natural resources. Although they have made some slight response to criticism, multilateral institutions continue their financial backing of large-scale "development" programmes even when they affect indigenous peoples' territories.

Where they have engaged with the national economy, indigenous peoples find themselves in a poor bargaining position at the bottom of the socio-economic pyramid. Ethnic and cultural differences often pit them against other deprived sectors of society such as the landless poor and migrant labourers. Clearly the traditional skills of indigenous peoples do not give them sufficient power to confront the external economy. The following sections discuss the skills they need to improve their bargaining position, how these skills are best acquired and the necessary relationship between traditional and newly-acquired skills. The transition will be painful, but the consequences of inaction are even more painful.

DISRUPTIVE INTERVENTIONS

I. Introduction

The forces of national society tend to undermine indigenous groups leaving them demoralised, impoverished and poorly placed to exert any control over their resources and their future. National or local development plans that institute or reinforce this tendency cannot be described as "development" for indigenous peoples. "Development" for them would mean a chance to determine their own future and their relations with the national society from a position of strength.

This section outlines strategies known to run counter to the interests of indigenous peoples. Sometimes the rights of indigenous peoples are simply ignored in the quest for national wealth, or sacrificed on grounds of the greater good. The ill effects are obvious, though frequently little recognised until the damage is done. Frequently, also, the "national interest" proves to be the interest only of a small elite.

But there exists also a range of schemes that harm indigenous interests much less obviously. They may even be presented as beneficial. Because fieldworkers need to be aware of the range of plans that can threaten the interests of indigenous peoples this section looks in some detail at negative experience.

II. Disruptive state intervention

1. State priorities

Not all state-sponsored action need by definition be negative, and some positive themes are considered in Section 3. Modern states have approached what they consider to be the "problem" of indigenous peoples in various ways, ranging from elimination by conquest at one extreme to isolation backed by the force of law at the other. Most states, but by no means all, now reject these extreme positions. Governments fear the international repercussions of genocide but are usually unwilling to sanction the "loss" of large land areas by guaranteeing their territory to an indigenous people. States are driven to intervene in the marginal areas occupied by indigenous people for all or some of the following reasons:

i. to assert the national culture, by suppressing indigenous religions and lifestyles. Communal dwellings are still being officially destroyed to teach indigenous peoples to live "morally" in nuclear families.
ii. to control the political frontier by taking physical possession.
iii. to extract natural resources.
iv. to offer a safety-valve for problem regions by finding "new" lands.

These priorities bring the state into direct conflict with the aspirations of the indigenous population for land and for a measure of independence within their territories. The state is often impatient with these aspirations and resentful of what it sees as backward populations spread at low density over strategic frontiers, and obstructing access to valuable resources while producing no taxable surplus. This leads it to adopt a range of damaging strategies.

2. Assimilation

The most common policies adopted to overcome these conflicts of interest rely on varying degrees of assimilation or integration into the dominant society and its economy. In practice, different peoples cannot be amalgamated without prejudice to the politically and economically weaker. All too often the exchange of an indigenous identity for a national one represents not "development", but a deterioration in the conditions and quality of life of indigenous peoples.

In the Gascoyne district of Western Australia, housing policy in Carnarvon seeks to assimilate Aborigines, interspersing selected Aborigines among white Australians and requiring them to live "white fashion". Those judged most acceptable to potential white neighbours are chosen, removing the most adaptable people from the reserve. Even so, adult men have no stake in town life; the Aboriginal town residents are women, children and the often unemployed young men; for mature men, town is simply a place to drink. Assimilation policies mean that the special department for Aborigines has been disbanded, and the provision of services for Aborigines is fully integrated. High unemployment, poor health, low incomes and alcoholism have not yielded to this well-meaning treatment.

3. Occupation

Colonial powers often created frontiers which divided indigenous territories. Many peoples in Amazonia and the Horn of Africa, for instance, found themselves separated from each other by new national allegiances.

Military forces responsible for maintaining national sovereignty in remote border areas are frankly distrustful of indigenous loyalties. Furthermore they generally discount local, traditional populations as an effective means of protecting national boundaries, and often choose policies that combine military possession with economic development. Large numbers of indigenous peoples have become refugees through conflicts, national and international, in which they have played no part. In some cases, they have sought to defend themselves against "development" and incurred terrible retribution. In others, they have been used as pawns: the San of Namibia, the Miskito of Nicaragua and the Montagnards of Laos and Vietnam all became puppets in conflicts of international significance. Some whole communities of the San and the Montagnards were deliberately moved into war zones; the Miskito, on the contrary, were moved out, with painful effects. "Living frontiers", where people are physically placed along the frontier, are one outcome of military interest.

The exact location of the northwest frontier of Peruvian Amazonia has been the subject of two wars with Ecuador over the last forty years. At stake are territory, oil and national pride. This is the territory of the Jivaro peoples, now divided between the Ecuadorian Shuar and the Aguaruna and Huambisa of Peru. Both governments maintain a strong military presence and encourage settlement by outsiders to the area in chains of purpose-built, heavily-subsidised townships known as "living frontiers". The indigenous peoples strongly resent the "development" of their territory by immigrants, arguing instead for investment in the existing population.

Brazil's Calha Norte (Northern Headwaters) Programme is similar; on the map, a string of farms owned by retired soldiers runs through the emptiness along the frontier. Citing the insecurity of a four-thousand-mile open frontier with six neighbouring states, the Brazilian military is planning to seal the frontier with a string of garrisons and to open up the Amazon to national economic exploitation in the interests of national security. Eight thousand Yanomami Indians who are pursuing legal recognition of their rights to part of this area stand to lose their traditional territory if Calha Norte is implemented.

4. Economic development
Among the most damaging strategies are those designed to increase the

productivity of an area inhabited by indigenous peoples. National governments and international funding agencies see the answer to socio-economic problems in national economic growth founded on greater exploitation of natural resources. Massive funding for infrastructure is often involved, with roads, bridges, pipelines and hydro-electric installations serving mines, oilfields, plantations and ranches. Patriotic calls to "expand the frontier" give governments an air of vigour and enterprise, and are strongly supported by bilateral and multilateral funding agencies as good examples of national initiative. But these investments have contributed to the enormous debts of many Third World countries and in most cases have not been shown to improve the conditions of the nation's poor, let alone of the indigenous people on whose land the "development" is carried out. National self-sufficiency in food may even be reduced.

The consequences of colonisation, relocation and sedentarisation are justified as the painful side-effects of action for the greatest good of the greatest number. Yet poverty and displacement have been brought about for the benefit of a wealthy minority. Destruction of weaker societies for the benefit of the stronger derives from a view of social evolution that is difficult to justify legally or theoretically.

i. Relocation. Removal of an indigenous group to another area is most commonly in the name of economic development: the potential returns for national elites and international finance may be very large. But on occasion, as with the Miskito in Nicaragua, the motive may be security.

In the Narmada Valley scheme, in India, two major dams will generate 2,700 megawatts of hydroelectricity, irrigate four to five million hectares, increase agricultural production by nearly 50% and supposedly benefit an estimated five million people. But 350,000 hectares will be flooded and, according to the National Institute of Urban Planning, an estimated one million people will eventually have to be resettled. One part of the scheme, the Sardar Sarovar Project, will displace 70,000 people, nearly all tribal, many of whom have no recognised legal title to the land (also a problem at Sobradinho and Tucurui, in Brazil). Though a resettlement and rehabilitation agreement has been drawn up, groups representing the oustees fear that promises made may never materialise. Many tribal systems of land tenure are not recognised by Indian law, as was the case with Australian law until 1976.

When resettlement schemes are planned and the original inhabitants are included in the process, the assumption is generally that they will benefit by incorporation into the national economy and dominant culture. It is tacitly or implicitly understood that the indigenous group will willingly sacrifice the larger part of its lands in exchange for the benefits of modernisation. This assumption denies ethnic pluralism and idealises a single national culture; weak as it is, it is often used as a justification for dispossession.

ii. Colonisation. When expansion into the lands of indigenous groups is justified in terms of "land for the landless" or, as in Brazil's state-sponsored colonisation of the tropical forest, of the relocation of "men without land to lands without men", the underlying objective is often to avoid more equitable distribution of assets in other areas of the country. Rather than antagonise the landowners, the state brings the rural poor into conflict with indigenous peoples. On other occasions, the state perceives colonisation as a cheap outlet for the unemployed of densely peopled regions; but in practice it is costly to secure sustained profit from colonisation. The Amazon has many examples.

Since 1981, with the help of some $500 million in loans from the World Bank, the Brazilian government's Polonoroeste Programme to colonise the west-central forest region has affected no less than sixty Indian groups, numbering nine thousand people. Extensive destruction of the forest has attracted international concern; most of the area cleared now supports only low-productivity cattle ranching. The forest is being mined, not developed.

At a cost of $550 million, met largely by the World Bank and the Inter American Development Bank, the Peruvian government launched a programme between 1981 and 1985 to relocate land-hungry peasants from the eroded highlands to the high jungle region. Much of the cost was road construction, linking the jungle to coastal markets. The programme affected most of the country's quarter of a million tropical forest Indians. The sacrifice of the indigenous people was for nothing, since in spite of the scale of investment and planning, the jungle soil cannot permanently yield agricultural surpluses without very close, skilled, long-term attention. No attempt was made to provide this.

Indigenous groups are also often ignored in programmes of "spontaneous" colonisation, where the state limits itself to funding roads. Any gains in production or employment will be at the direct cost of the indigenous population, particularly where no advance provision is made to

16

demarcate and protect their lands. Short-term increases in production are often illusory, as the unplanned expansion of the agricultural frontier has grave environmental side-effects and much land is permanently damaged. Even soils which could, with sufficient skills and inputs, sustain production rarely receive them in colonisation areas.

iii. Sedentarisation. Like enforced isolation, relocation and colonisation, sedentarisation is often presented as being in the interests of indigenous people. The real concern of the state is usually with control, as when Indian reservations were created in the United States. For many low-income countries, sedentarisation of nomads is official policy; they are perceived as a threat to national security and national culture. The good intentions of the state are little protection: in Tanzania, the concentration of population into villages was intended not only to promote economic growth but to make it easier to deliver services. The nomadic Hadza, who had not previously needed the principles of hygiene essential for settled group life, were soon devastated by disease. In Botswana, it has turned out to be no cheaper to provide services for the new nucleated villages than for the old scattered homesteads.

The efficiency of traditional nomadic and semi-nomadic systems depended heavily on household mobility, for following game, for using distant pastures or for escaping pests and disease. That efficiency can be restored: a way of delivering services to shifting encampments is sorely needed, for these are viable and productive societies with much to teach. Kindness, generosity, consideration, affection, honesty, hospitality, compassion and charity — these have been described as not virtues but necessities for survival for foraging peoples. They are a great deal to lose in the interest of "national security".

The Ik once hunted and gathered in the mountains between Uganda, Kenya and Sudan. Much time was spent in the Kidepo Valley in Uganda: when this was lost to a national park, they were settled as farmers. Other government intervention was largely confined to confiscating their spears and trying to persuade them to wear clothes. The Ik were reduced to living off badly administered government relief, poaching, prostitution or thieving. Famine followed, with an attendant and horrifying social collapse.

Family ties which had once been strong simply ceased to exist among the Ik, and much else with them. No evidence of love, affection or self-sacrifice could be identified. The young and relatively healthy, (say fifteen to nineteen year olds) consciously ensured that hunger was confined first to the

17

aged, then, as hunger worsened, to the children. Everyone took food from others by force, even from the mouths of their parents and children. Anyone who could not take care of themselves was a burden and a hazard to the survival of others. The young and active, when they obtained famine relief, consumed it themselves. A dispensary where the old as well as the young received food and medicine was regared as immoral and wasteful. Grief and mourning almost disappeared, as did formal burial; callousness to physical and mental suffering reached the point where the misfortune of others became a pleasure.

Yet, before the establishment of the national park, the Ik seemed to have been as socially responsible as other foragers. Such persistent and extreme behavioural changes are now recognised as characteristic human reactions to prolonged semi-starvation.

iv. Technical change. Intervention directed at raising the "productivity" of indigenous societies can also be destructive. All too often planners assume that the problems of small-scale, subsistence societies are primarily economic and result from inadequate technologies. They frequently design interventions without even consulting the group concerned, or troubling to find out how production is linked to social relations within the group, or even what production is for. "Improvements" to African pastoralism have often assumed that production of animals for sale is the main objective; yet the optimal age and sex structures of herds and flocks are quite different when the animals are for consumption as meat, and different again when the main product is milk.

By concentrating on the market economy to the exclusion of everything else, advisers tend to destabilise traditional societies and undermine their subsistence. As has been seen in Section 1, a subsistence-based society is likely to maintain its social relations by consumption through sharing. Generosity within the group may be given a higher priority than individual accumulation. The redistribution of surplus production tends to be institutionalised and will have direct bearing on the way authority is measured or exercised. Among egalitarian societies, technological innovation may lead to inequalities; similarly, individual modes of ownership may hinder collective activity. Programmes designed solely for the economy may not only be socially destructive, but may also tend to diminish local control and promote dependence on the market.

The ultimate aim of intervention is often to encourage a change to sedentary, market-oriented practices more typical of peasants. The creation of agricultural surpluses for the national or regional market conflicts with the traditional indigenous preoccupation with minimising risks. Risks will nevertheless increase rather than diminish as relations with national society intensify.

Failure to understand the ecological balance can also lead to disaster. The provision of water for nomadic pastoralists has led to devastation and famine when it has disrupted traditional controls and promoted overstocking. The replacement of rainforest by low-productivity cattle ranching damages soils, promotes flooding and erosion and may reduce rainfall. Indigenous groups are skilled at surviving extreme conditions; few technical schemes for semi-arid lands allow for very dry years. In Africa, local pastoral systems were based on opportunistic movement, multiple species, and browsing, not grazing, in the dry season: incoming knowledge had little to say that was relevant.

Using World Bank credit, the Aguaruna of the Alto Mayo in Peru embarked on large-scale levelling, ditching and planting of wet rice on portions of their forest lands, using a combination of advanced technology for clearing and ditching and intensive manual labour for transplanting. Costly mistakes led to immense debts which provoked serious internal differences in the communities. One community found itself embroiled in a dispute over a caterpillar tractor acquired for forest clearing and levelling. The machine seized up within a month of purchase but accrued arrears of interest for several years before it could be sold. Inappropriate technology and credit threaten to overwhelm Aguaruna community structures.

In 1974, a colonisation scheme at Uxpanapa in Mexico was designed to resettle Indians displaced by construction of a dam. Heavy equipment and new collective forms of labour and ownership were to produce rice for the market. The technology was untried; the new varieties of rice succumbed to the effects of high rainfall, as did the combine harvesters; the Indians had to harvest by hand. The expensive equipment was soon withdrawn, and the communal experiment collapsed into individual farms.

5. Inappropriate services

States with limited resources for rural services such as health, education and agricultural support rarely extend these to the members of indigenous societies. Even when services are provided, they may be a mixed blessing.

Services may be imposed in authoritarian and unsympathetic ways, may be culturally unacceptable, may alienate the people from their traditions, may undermine existing practices and may create unnecessary dependence.

Services designed to change societies to fit the ideological requirements of the state are unlikely to be beneficial. State education generally arrives in a marginal area ahead of health services: this is an indication that it is seen as a tool of acculturation.

Educational policy at national level may be progressive, incorporating minority languages and allowing for the training of indigenous teachers. But, unless there is recognition also of the need for modifications to the curriculum and teaching methodology, this system may amount to no more than a sophisticated means of controlling indigenous populations. Salaried teachers, for instance, tend to establish an elite within collective societies and their ultimate allegiance may lie outside the group. Bilingual systems may be just another form of acculturation when literacy training in the mother tongue is merely a route to the national culture.

The state is often insensitive to differences between groups. In Peru, new laws in the 1970s offered real opportunities to indigenous peoples, but assumed incorrectly that the jungle peoples also had the concept of a territorial, self-governing community characteristic of the highland Quechua.

III. Disruption from the wider economy
National economy and society may disrupt indigenous lives without specific government plans.

1. Land and labour as commodities
In the national economy, labour and land are commodities. This conception is completely alien to indigenous societies, and the introduction of commercial relationships in these spheres may threaten their whole society.

2. Undermining subsistence economies
Fragile environments have been disturbed and their inhabitants eventually impoverished by the assumption that systems of production directed towards local needs are inefficient and must be intensified or transformed. From the point of view of indigenous societies, the more urgent need is to develop the means of defending their lands and the traditional use of them. Market-oriented agriculture, promoted at the expense of subsistence production, often does not guarantee sufficient income to purchase food, so nutrition may be severely reduced. As more land is dedicated to cash crops or cattle ranching, consumer crops become scarce and their prices

are inflated; once-plentiful sources of protein in forests and rivers disappear. Wage labour may similarly take essential time from subsistence production without enabling people to buy the goods foregone.

The viability of subsistence economies may be undermined by governments that only allow land rights to indigenous peoples on condition that they increase productivity. Presented with the choice of losing their lands to settlers or converting the forest to commercial agriculture, the Shuar of Ecuador have become large-scale cattle breeders. Many Shuar communities now face hunger since the conversion of forest to pasture has made slash and burn agriculture impossible and game has disappeared with the forest.

3. Altering gender roles
Many indigenous groups have marked sexual division of labour. Roles vary greatly between groups; among some peoples women are thought too clumsy to sew. It is usually women who cultivate subsistence crops, gather wild fruits and insects, carry heavy loads and are responsible for domestic duties; and often it is men and boys who hunt or herd large animals, or clear land for cultivation. In most societies women do more work, but the complementarity of men's and women's roles make each sex dependent on the other. Gender roles are culturally prescribed and often remain unquestioned by either sex until external circumstances upset the balance. At present, all national societies are highly patriarchal: whatever their own gender roles and relations, indigenous peoples must relate to a wider society in which women lack power and in which their work is unrecognised. Commercial and other contacts then tend to disrupt the indigenous gender roles and relations, to the disadvantage of the whole society, but often particularly of the women.

Disruption of the subsistence base can bear heavily on women. In hunting, herding and horticultural societies, men may contribute a significant part of the animal protein. This may be lost by loss of lands or by the diversion of men into migrant labour, casual employment or cash cropping. Whatever the circumstances, the onus of subsistence falls increasingly on the woman. In nomadic and semi-nomadic African societies men often move away in search of work when animals die in a drought. In Amazonia, the family must be fed entirely from the garden, which the woman now maintains alone; poultry and livestock introduced to compensate for lack of game will also be her responsibility. Worldwide, if the man is cash-cropping he may require the woman to help him, and will probably set apart the best lands available for his new crops rather than for the subsistence garden. Women's traditional land rights may disappear. Contact with national society may make women dependent agricultural workers; they may still do the greater part of the work, but have little or no control over how the cash earned is spent. The status of women suffers, for instance, when their subsistence horticulture loses place to market agriculture in which men make decisions, if only because this is the rule in the national society. When cash is injected into traditional societies, the artefacts and beverages produced by the women lose prestige. Women may give up making these things, and they may gradually be replaced by purchased manufactured items. At first, the amount of women's work may appear to be reduced when they need no longer weave clothing, make clay pots and other utensils; but women may be losing control over productive areas of their lives.

Some of the Karamoja of Uganda were resettled by an NGO (non-governmental organisation) during a famine after losing their cattle to armed raiders. The project set out to establish families in better environments as independent, self-supporting farmers. In the traditional economy, the men's economic roles focussed on cattle, the women's on agriculture. Since all the cattle had been lost, the new agricultural livelihood meant that men must find new roles. Traditionally, the male roles were in the dry-season grazing territory and the cattle camp, while the women built, cleaned and maintained the family dwelling, cultivated, planted, weeded and harvested the crops, brought the harvest home, stored it, milled the grain, collected firewood and water, cooked, brewed beer and cared for children. The men will have to make drastic adjustments if they are to redirect their enormous energy, but they have made little progress. They are beginning to undertake some clearing of fields, digging of holes for planting, and some harvesting but they still accept leisure while most work falls on their wives and daughters. The need to involve men in farm work or household duties is critical if food production is to be successful in the resettlement area.

4. Exploitation of new needs

Indigenous groups suddenly introduced to plentiful supplies of trade goods and manufactured articles are vulnerable to exploitation when they lack the regular income necessary to satisfy the newly felt needs for them.

As a result of an effort to expedite social change among the Ashaninca of Peru, members of a mission-based community acquired both a strong desire for commercial goods and a strong aversion to engaging in any productive activity to earn the means of acquiring them. As the settler economy of the valley developed a heavy bias towards drug trafficking, the Ashaninca of the mission community were drawn into paid work, providing services for the traffickers and exposing themselves unwittingly to later reprisals.

IV. Disruptive activities of non-governmental organisations

Interventions harmful to indigenous people are not limited to large-scale, internationally financed programmes; they can also be implemented by NGOs. Each of the many NGOs operating on behalf of indigenous peoples has its own approach. The NGO's approach is always more personal than the transformation of the environment carried out by the larger state projects, yet it may be nearly as disruptive. Many NGOs employ a common methodology based on work at community level and with emphasis on participation and self-reliance; their particular goals will determine the nature of the intervention and its effect on the indigenous group. There are several areas in which interventions by NGOs can be damaging to indigenous people.

1. Ideological imposition

Schemes tailored to the interests of the NGO rather than the beneficiaries may have as their underlying objective the imposition of a particular religious, economic or political doctrine. The position of confidence enjoyed by some church groups within countries with indigenous populations has often given them a free hand to plan and implement change for the groups with which they work. Church groups can be tempted to encourage indigenous peoples to establish relations of extreme dependence, particularly where there is competition between sects. Where the over-riding priority is religious conversion, all other aspects may be subordinated to this goal. The insensitive imposition of alien religions on indigenous peoples can destroy them.

Similarly, NGOs with a strong political stance may be tempted to impose political ideologies, dividing indigenous organisations over ends and interests that are not their own and even provoking reprisals. These reprisals are often directed as much against the indigenous people, who may or may not have understood the implications of their actions, as against the NGO. Members of an NGO who contemplate an intervention among indigenous peoples that involves political action need to be extremely careful.

A fundamentalist Christian sect based in Florida faces international criticism on many counts. They have shown contempt for indigenous culture, their educational work has been ethnocidal, destroying culture, they have illegally issued tokens redeemable only at the mission store as payment for indigenous labour and they have failed to support indigenous campaigns for land rights. As a result, members of one tribe, the Ayoreo, now live mainly at isolated mission stations in Bolivia. Few stations have schools; those that do, teach from biblical texts in the Indian language, withholding practical skills and the language and culture of national society. In the city of Santa Cruz, runaway Ayoreo families beg in the main square while Ayoreo girls contract venereal disease as prostitutes around the railway station.

An NGO with left-wing sympathies, working with the Cocamilla in the Huallaga Valley of Peru in 1984, encouraged the native organisation to strike against discriminatory credit practices by the state Agrarian Bank. The unfortunate end result of this action was that members of both the NGO and the indigenous organisation were exposed to serious harassment, including imprisonment and torture, when unrelated subversive violence in the area led to a government crackdown on all forms of community organisation.

2. Conflict

Where NGOs with contrasting or contradictory approaches are in the same area, competition can become a source of divisions that may persist long after the departure of the NGOs. This has occurred all over the Amazon region, where generally conservative and long established mission interests clash with new, secular NGOs. The two sides struggle for influence over the indigenous group, often creating, maintaining and supporting rival indigenous leaders. Even after the NGOs and the missionaries withdraw from an area, indigenous leadership struggles are indelibly altered.

3. Paternalism

Even initiatives supposedly geared to the interests of the people will tend to establish paternalistic relations of dependence if they are planned, executed and/or directed by NGO staff and if there is no commitment to the phasing out of external advisers, or insufficient stress on training. The indigenous group will be lulled into a false sense of security, and the eventual departure of the NGO will leave it as vulnerable as it was before the intervention.

The particular vulnerability of indigenous peoples has exposed them to well-intentioned programmes that undertake to redefine their lives on the assumption that they are not capable of managing their own affairs. Indigenous peoples can sometimes profit from emergency attention, but many long-term programmes of support are based on preconceptions of indigenous incapacity which may become self-fulfilling. A people judged to be unable to take responsibility for its own survival may well become permanently dependent on outside support.

i. Institutional paternalism. The state is guilty of paternalism where indigenous peoples are classified as minors and subject to the tutelage of government institutions. Paternalism also occurs where indigenous peoples are entrusted to the care of missions which see themselves as guardians and educators with control and authority over all aspects of the people's lives. Even NGO fieldworkers encouraging self-reliance through participation may also be guilty of paternalism if they impose their advice on the group or, more insidiously, use their own knowledge and experience to sway opinions and decisions.

ii. Ethnocentric attitudes. Fieldworkers' own culture will condition their opinions of the societies with which they are involved. If they have a restricted, ethnocentric view it will colour their assessment of possibilities and define the changes they advocate. For the sake of positive and visible achievements, fieldworkers with little self-awareness can be guilty of encouraging changes to fit the priorities of their own culture. A fieldworker who assumes, for instance, that the subordination of women is a priority area for change, may well not be responding to need as felt by the group — by either women or men. Ethnocentrism is never entirely avoidable between non-native change agent and indigenous group but every fieldworker needs to be aware of the dangers, to take care to gain a thorough understanding of the people and their priorities and to respect the people's decisions even when they conflict with the fieldworker's own views.

iii. Ignoring indigenous skills. Paternalism is also present where indigenous culture and knowledge are assumed to be qualititatively inferior to, rather than different from, that of the majority culture. Outsiders often see their role as a "civilising" one, uncritically regarding their own skills as superior or more appropriate. This form of paternalism, and the relationships it brings about, can be among the most debilitating. Almost every project with indigenous people in the jungles of Peru has sought to introduce temperate vegetables to people who are expert gardeners of their own indigenous crops. Such programmes are debilitating, not only because they take up indigenous people's time, but also because they sap their confidence, discrediting their knowledge.

iv. Gift-giving This is one of the most obvious forms of paternalism. People accustomed to receiving on request medicine, food, tools, seed or livestock will lose the ability to improve their lives through their own efforts. During famine in the Sudan, there were several cases of fishermen in coastal villages (whose livelihood was unaffected) stopping fishing as long as food aid was available. The Nandeva of Paraguay have come to speak of "hunting aid" as a skill. When crises arise, there is always a temptation for relatively articulate indigenous groups to ask for (and NGOs to give) short-term assistance. Care must be taken to identify the real causes of the problem and, if possible, to support the group with long-term solutions. The Shipibo in Peru are suffering from increasingly frequent floods, caused by deforestation outside their territory. Help comes from the NGOs which promote agricultural change, not from those which supply food aid. Even in a full scale disaster,such as recent African famines, the subsequent independence of the group must be a priority.

It is not possible to avoid the problem by having a ruling not to give gifts. For many peoples, gift-giving is the local way of creating social relationships with non-kin; an exchange of gifts may demonstrate equality; refusal of gifts may be perceived as hostile, inadequate behaviour. Great sensitivity is required.

v. Benevolent despotism. Paternalism may be less obvious in programmes that are designed to promote self-reliance but are planned and carried out by outside advisers. Just as giving gifts may encourage dependence, so does doing for people things they are able to do themselves — or can learn to do themselves. Even if the goals of the programme meet the needs of the people, this will not help them to manage their own change in the future, unless they actively participate. Fieldworkers must avoid being cast in the role of programme managers.

vi. Conclusion. Paternalism bedevils work with indigenous peoples. Thought must be given to the many ways it can arise, and active steps must be taken to avoid it, otherwise programmes are likely either to fail or to breed dependence. Many long-term programmes, particularly missions, simply ignore the paternalist nature of their work.

Throughout Amazonia, indigenous groups have become accustomed to patrons who provide for the Indians' needs in return for labour or products. This customary relationship of dependence or debt-bondage can be psychological as well as financial and sometimes induces Indian peoples to recreate the same system with fieldworkers who are seeking to

promote self-reliance. When the fieldworker attempts to compete with patrons for the Indians' loyalty, or gives free rein to his or her own need to feel wanted and respected, a mockery is made of any attempt to free the people from their bonds.

The frequently deep-seated nature of indigenous dependence makes it difficult to show that self-reliance is better than the short-term economic benefits of relations with a patron. Many projects therefore fail, and indigenous people may reject projects which encourage self-reliance. There are also cases where people make the conscious, informed decision to choose the path of assimilation into national society, whatever the cost. Fieldworkers who cannot accept their decision are themselves guilty of paternalism.

4. Selectivity
Lack of staff often compels NGOs to limit support to those indigenous groups that can manage their own changes largely unassisted. The result may be short-term over-funding of a few favoured groups rather than the risk of a long-term commitment to support with no ultimate guarantee of success. Groups that are known for their failures with community projects, and are therefore unattractive to funding agencies, are paradoxically those most in need of well-thought-out, patient and far-reaching NGO support. Unfortunately, NGOs tend to shy away from this sort of high risk group.

5. Changes in gender relations
Measures intended to strengthen the bargaining power of an indigenous group, such as community and inter-community organisations, may exclude women and render them subordinate. While good education and training prepare men to confront change from a position of strength, programmes for women tend to be limited to cookery, manual crafts and sewing. Conversely, difficulties arise from the targeting of women as an oppressed group within indigenous groups that are themselves oppressed: there may be considerable cultural opposition to a more equitable sharing of power and status.

6. Power brokers
Indigenous people find their way of life under threat. Their traditional knowledge, tools and systems cannot cope: they need to acquire new skills and knowledge, and this brings them into contact with a variety of brokers or intermediaries. Indigenous groups have learnt that every offer of assistance is subject to conditions, and a major function of indigenous leadership is to discern the hidden agenda. Institutions with vested

interests are strongly tempted to take advantage of indigenous vulnerability. State agencies wishing to control indigenous populations and their resources, and missionaries with sectarian interests, both seek to identify and support new leaders who can be trained to be more amenable than the traditional leadership. There is a temptation to work with a younger generation which has had primary schooling and has probably acquired non-traditional skills such as literacy, necessary for the self-management of a viable health, education or economic programme. Work with the young raises three main issues.

i. It may exacerbate existing power struggles between the young and old.

ii. By the transfer of power from older, "traditional" people to the younger, more "modern" group, a traditional culture may be supplanted in as little as one generation.

iii. A project that focusses exclusively on the younger generation may not only alienate the older generation, but also may itself become a subject of power struggles within the group; its end result could be to divide and weaken the group.

7. Haste
Since one strength of indigenous groups lies in the integration of social, political and economic aspects of their societies, rapid change in any one area will affect the whole and weaken the links that bind the society together. The time required for social change must be allowed, because rushed interventions will fail. When haste is excessive, the slow assimilation of new ideas is easily confused with apathy and increasingly coercive or paternalistic measures may be adopted to achieve short-term project goals.

V. Snags of self-determination
Although this manual recommends that the most appropriate type of change for indigenous people is that designed, implemented and managed by the people themselves, it is important to warn fieldworkers against some common misconceptions on self-management. Self-determination, for instance, when applied to indigenous peoples rarely amounts to full recognition of their rights to occupy their own territory in the way they feel best, and rarely guarantees them freedom from molestation. It more often means the right to take up a place defined by legislation in national society. In South America, self-determination has come to be synonymous with positive indigenous change; yet it may not succeed.

1. Dissent
Projects that seek to create autonomous institutions among people that

have not recognised a need for them may succeed only in multiplying their difficulties. They may cause internal dissent; the concentration of new forms of authority in fewer hands may create elites, or funds and authority may be misused for personal profit or prestige.

In Peru the 1974 law on behalf of the country's quarter of a million forest peoples favoured self-management of indigenous change. By granting legal recognition to individual communities and acknowledging their right to self-government within specific territorial limits, the state accepted a compromise over the use of territories occupied by indigenous groups that gave them considerable potential to change — on a path of their own. During the 1970s, organisations sprang up in every corner of the Peruvian jungle to take advantage of the new law. However many of these were created by government anthropologists rather than by the people themselves. As long as methods were not coercive, the indigenous people were content to cooperate in the hope of receiving land titles. But genuine organisations that would go on to manage marketing, health and education were rare. In the most extreme cases, organisations became dominated by charismatic figures who used them to reinforce their own positions and gain for themselves national and international reputations.

2. Blocking projects

The new leadership of organisations may reject programmes which the people want but which offer no material gain to the leaders themselves. A handicraft marketing programme initiated on behalf of the Ashaninca communities of the River Tambo in Peru was welcomed by the producers but community leaders were not enthusiastic when they learnt that the capital of the project could not be used by their organisation to cover running expenses.

3. Corruption

Self-managed change in the economic sphere is particularly difficult to achieve unless accompanied by effective training programmes and accountability for funds. Indigenous organisations that interpret self-management as the right to claim funds but deny any accountability are abusing the concept; far from achieving the desired independence, they become dependent on handouts. Leaders of this type have even been bribed into offering the support of the organisation to dispossess member-communities of their lands. "Leaders" imposed from outside who are not locally accountable may be highly problematic.

Among the Beja of the Sudan, high level leaders were a creation of government, never recognised in traditional society. NGOs have found that some of them represent the interests of their people for no personal gain, some do so for a high price, and others are totally self-interested. In the district of Sinkat, the World Food Programme distributed famine relief through these "big" sheiks. The district is mountainous, the people are migrant, widely dispersed and divided into numerous subtribes. This segmentation has been a successful adaptation, with complex land rights that control access to water, grazing, wood cutting and cultivation, but food distribution in a mass famine seemed impossible. Only the sheiks, it was said, could know how many people were where. The food was freighted to delivery points where the sheiks were to organise distribution. Many of them loaded the food back onto the truck and sold it in the towns, particularly the oil, sugar and milk. After intervention by an NGO, the responsibility was moved from town-based sheiks to local men, popularly nominated leaders. (Monitoring was carried out by women travelling round the households.) Distribution proved equitable: excessively so, since most leaders insisted on equal handouts to all households, regardless of size or wealth.

4. The loss of intermediary groups

Direct funding of indigenous organisations may seem to be better than funding through an intermediary centre. It may avoid paternalism, and the indigenous organisation seems the best qualified to identify and initiate projects within its area.Yet it may be preferable at first to entrust finance to professionals in intermediary centres, if they have a genuine commitment to train leaders and to phase themselves out. Truly effective self-managed change has emerged in Peru only after long periods of preparation by intermediaries. The Aguaruna people of the Alto Maranon, for example, succeeded in forming a solid, representative organisation after ten years of intensive effort by a Spanish intermediary group. Similarly the Shuar Federation of Ecuador — perhaps the most vigorous and effective of all South American indigenous organisations — received a basic grounding in the principles of self-management from Salesian missionaries.

5. Conclusion

The successful promotion of social change in indigenous groups depends on the programme and the pace of change. Rather than rush into a project, it is better to take a conservative view of the time needed to reach a proper understanding of peoples' needs, always planning for more rather than less time to meet specific goals. Fieldworkers should bear in mind the need for a flexible approach that takes into account the possibility of constant revision and replanning by the people themselves.

CONDITIONS FOR SUCCESS

I. Introduction

What programmes can help indigenous peoples to gain more control over their own lives? What processes can overcome their isolation from decisions? What approaches can reinforce their cultural identity and enable them to resist assimilation on unfavourable terms? Each people reacts differently and each situation calls for a particular response from the NGO. Within one multi-ethnic country the variety can be very wide, and the temptation to design common solutions needs to be resisted. Yet there are some common themes.

II. Self-management

Instances of successful self-management occur widely, but particularly in Western Amazonia, Canada and Australia.

1. Organisation

Practical work with indigenous peoples has, until recently, tended to concentrate on modifying the indigenous economy towards production for the market, perhaps with some provision of services such as health and education. The effect has often been to create or perpetuate dependence and to stultify any attempt by indigenous people to make their own decisions. Projects promoting self-management of change will require at least as much emphasis on new forms of organisation as on production or services. This calls for great skill in finding the correct balance: awareness must be aroused, organisations formed and social and economic needs met, without the creation of dependence.

2. Political representation

This is the key. If they are to plan, implement and effectively control their own future, indigenous groups need to evolve representative organisations that reflect their own aspirations; these must implement programmes that meet their needs, and must also achieve some form of legal recognition. Without representation, indigenous peoples find themselves in a weak position when subjected to social, economic and legal abuses. It may seem ethnocentric to specify representation when traditional systems may have been very different, but the present situation is different again, since indigenous people must engage with national society. Efforts by NGOs that ignore the lack of political voice will not touch the fundamental problems.

i. Deploy consensus. Self-management calls on the potential for organisation inherent in the group's traditional sense of common identity and solidarity. However, there is wide variation in the degree of solidarity felt by indigenous peoples. Many do identify themselves as a group by virtue of ancestry, language, culture or territorial possession. Other, traditionally loose, indigenous societies may be much fragmented, perhaps originally as an adaptation to scarce resources.

ii. Transcend traditional divisions. Even the most deeply divided groups can acquire the skills necessary to present a common institutional front. A sense of ethnic identity may even be created by the perception that others share one's predicament, as when wider groupings of the Cree emerged to combat the general threat of the James Bay Hydroelectric Scheme in Canada.

In Peru the strongest organisation representing the rights of lowland Indian peoples has been developed by the indigenous group with traditionally the most serious internal rivalries. The Aguaruna and Huambisa Council brings together nearly a hundred communities that until recently were plagued by internal warfare exacerbated by a tradition of revenge killing. The Aguaruna and Huambisa recognised the ineffectiveness of their traditions against external threats and rechannelled their bellicosity through an institution which by its combative spirit has earned room to manoeuvre within the national political context.

iii. Open channels of communication. All successful self-managed indigenous organisations hold a regular (usually annual) meeting of representatives at which strategies are determined and needs expressed. It is also during these meetings that contact is established between the indigenous people and the representatives of the government departments whose policies affect their lives and that terms are negotiated with supporting NGOs.

3. Intermediaries

In Peru, as in the rest of South America, self-management has initially required the support of concerned professionals and intermediary groups. Success will depend heavily at first on the perceptions of the professionals,

Guami People, Ecuador

Mike Goldwater, Network

'All successfully self-managed indigenous organisations hold a regular (usually annual) meeting of representatives at which strategies are determined and needs expressed.' (page 33).

their previous experience, the skills they bring to the task and their understanding of the specific potential of the group.

For the Aguaruna and Huambisa people, self-management emerged from nine years of effort by an intermediary organisation of Spanish professionals, the Development of the Upper Maranon (DAM). On successful completion of the project, the leader commented that the many practical projects (including a wide range of agricultural, health and marketing initiatives) were primarily a means to an end.The objective was to inspire in the people a critical view of the options offered by the essentially paternalistic church groups that had worked in the area for several decades. DAM had estimated that it would take ten years for the people to establish an organisation of their own, but this was achieved in nine, when the Aguaruna Council became strong enough to dispense with DAM's services. Since then the Council has confronted many difficulties in planning and implementing change but in its relations with non-indigenous people of every description — officials, missionaries, professionals and settlers — there is no doubt either of the supremacy of the annual assembly of representatives in deciding priorities, or of the solidarity of the member communities with their elected Council.

4. Isolated groups

The effectiveness of self-management depends at least in part on the quality of the preparation. Indigenous groups that have little or no experience of national society will tend to require a much longer period of groundwork before they realise the need to break free of dependence and initiate organisations as sophisticated as the Aguaruna and Huambisa Council. It may be easier for such people to organise initially around a single issue such as land titling. Imposing organisation does not work and should in no circumstances be attempted. These groups will only gradually see the necessity of organisation for confronting national society. They may gain confidence in learning to administer (for example) small scale marketing programmes that serve their needs.

III. Meeting felt needs

Most "indigenous development" has attempted to impose false needs. The ideology was the outmoded view of human evolution as an escalator of progress from "savage" nomadism to settled "civilisation". This manual does not explain how to "civilise" people, but rather how to assist a particular group at a given time to identify and meet real needs. It argues that the most effective method is through indigenous organisations. The task of the change agent is to listen, discuss and then encourage. Groups which are able to participate in supplying their own felt needs gain confidence in self-management.

1. Identify priorities

The aim must be to respond to priority needs, as expressed by the people, rather than to introduce models devised by outsiders. The goal should not be to solve all their problems immediately, even if this is a temptation when a group is found to be facing land shortages, poor education and minimal provision for health, but rather to locate an area of their lives on which they feel they can improve.

2. Meet needs

If projects identify needs in this way, they will generate high levels of enthusiasm and participation. Because people understand the goals and have identified them themselves, they will do something to achieve them. Much of the work of agricultural extension, for instance, being done in the Third World has such a low rate of success because it seeks to impose techniques and activities on people who are unconvinced. Many techniques are inappropriate in any terms; some are merely poorly presented and simply not perceived as fulfilling a requirement.

When it comes to meeting the needs identified, the change agent becomes a resource. He or she may be able to help with technical information, or credit, or, very probably, with knowledge of national society and its institutions. This will help the group to form representative institutions that can apply pressure on the authorities to provide services, for example, and that can effectively manage these services. Training must be arranged to ensure that necessary skills are acquired.

It is vital to realise that participation in national society is a skill that must be learnt. The indigenous institutions formed to meet needs will vary greatly. Apathetic groups that have difficulty in defining their needs will be unlikely to form elaborate institutions for cooperation and self-defence. Yet these people are often those most in need of mutual aid. Ad hoc groups formed with a specific purpose, such as the building of a bridge or a schoolhouse, may give them confidence and lay the foundations for future participation on a wider scale.

3. Conclusion

Ideally the kind of discussion recommended here is a continual learning process for both the indigenous group and the change agent. It will help people to appreciate the strength of their own culture as a tool of change. Plans may still go wrong for many reasons, some of which are discussed in Section 5, but success is far more likely than if solutions are imposed. Indigenous groups have great ability to adapt forms of organisation and production.

IV. Restoring confidence

1. The problem
One of the most serious obstacles to self-management as a goal for indigenous people is their own acceptance of the low opinion of them expressed by members of the national society. Strong discrimination against subsistence economies, minority languages and indigenous forms of dress will often cause indigenous groups to suppress these differences and to adopt as far as possible the appearance and attributes of the dominant culture. This often leads, after a generation or two, to a group forgetting its own culture and knowledge. The resulting "cultural amnesia" can be the backbone of a group's lack of confidence. Indigenous groups that retain a positive sense of their own worth are well placed to resist external pressures. They do not seek to transform themselves totally, but aim to acquire those skills they feel are necessary to support their traditional lifestyle. Many activities may promote confidence.

2. Positive action
To guarantee a people's rights to its resources is a fundamental step towards preserving a sense of self-worth. In addition, outsiders may:
i. help to identify areas of need in which quick success is likely.
ii. fight "cultural amnesia" by rediscovering with people the value of their own traditional skills and knowledge. A European scientist engaged in research and voluntary work was the catalyst for the Shipibo, in Peru, to rediscover the value of their medical expertise.
iii. ensure that education reflects local reality and incorporates traditions.
iv. write down oral histories and organise indigenous radio programmes.
v. encourage meetings and help people to organise and conduct general meetings at group level.
vi. support contacts between indigenous groups.
vii. promote crafts by providing secure markets for them.

Crafts, even where they were not traditional, have reinforced indigenous identity and confidence. For instance, carving is an introduced art form among the Canadian Eskimo; souvenir crafts and children's toys led in the 1960s to a flourishing art

37

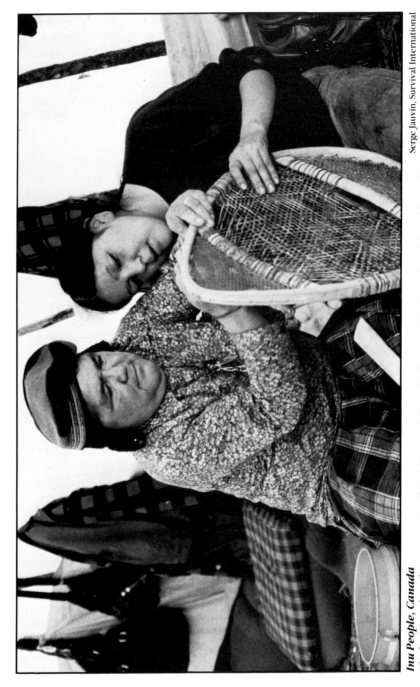

Innu People, Canada
'Crafts, even where they were not traditional, have reinforced indigenous identity and confidence.' (page 37).

Serge Jauvin, Survival International

form which has replaced hunting as the main livelihood and personal satisfaction of many Eskimo adults. They say they would prefer to hunt, or to engage in regular wage labour, but meanwhile the income is valued, and craft co-operatives, together with consumer and housing co-operatives, have become the social and political foci of community and regional development in most of the Canadian Arctic. Similarly, the Ainu of Japan also lost the economic security based on traditional resources; tourist art has provided new sources of employment, economic networks and sociopolitical roles.

Many groups use crafts to emphasise shared beliefs and group membership.

Early in this century, the Cuna in Panama were being forcibly assimilated. They fought for and achieved some autonomy, and, as part of their rebellion, they emphasised traditional dress for women. This dress had developed since contact; the "mola" blouse is less than 100 years old, but now is a source of family pride, an expressive outlet for the women and one of the Cuna's main sources of cash. Molas are made to be worn by the Cuna women, and are usually sold only after their wearers are tired of them. Cuna ethnicity is closely tied to a Cuna woman's standard dress form.

3. Discrimination

An important aspect of self-confidence is the willingness of indigenous people to oppose pressures by national or international opinion which denigrate their cultures, traditions and histories.

The self confidence of the Cuna is well illustrated by their reaction to a rumour that the Peace Corps had brought sewing machines and taught the women how to make molas. At first they thought it amusing, because they had sewing machines long before they had Peace Corps volunteers; later, they became angry at the idea that they would do as they were told in such a field, and wrote to the New York Times, one source of the original rumour.

When in 1979 the German film-maker Werner Herzog arrived in Peru to produce his version of the life of Fitzcarrald, a turn of the century rubber baron, the Aguaruna Council took a firm stand against its filming in indigenous territory. Indians refused to participate in a myth in which one of the wealthiest and most bloodthirsty rubber merchants was represented as a considerate and eccentric music-lover obsessed with the dream of bringing opera to the Amazon. Herzog and his team were expelled from the Aguaruna area and a national debate was provoked in Congress that polarised opinion around a reassessment of the country's national heroes. The Aguaruna insisted, and were able to persuade public opinion, that men who had built fortunes on slavery and the elimination of tens of thousands of indigenous people did not bring glory to Peru, but shame. During the protracted dispute all work for change in Aguaruna territory came to a standstill, but the indigenous Council emerged victorious and greatly strengthened. Herzog did not abandon his plans but transferred the film team a thousand miles south to Ashaninca territory. The Ashaninca did not have the organisational experience, the political awareness or the desire to frustrate his plans. Herzog was able to establish a relationship of traditional patronage with large numbers of Ashaninca, with whom the film was eventually completed.

V. Allowing time

Innovations, however appropriate, may become disruptive in themselves unless indigenous groups have time to absorb them. Just how much time is necessary will depend on a number of factors, including above all whether the group wishes to change and whether it perceives the need to do so.

1. Emergencies

Emergencies call for rapid responses, whether they are caused by earthquake, famine or the disruptive impact of a new mine or road. It must be remembered that an emergency programme needs always to be extremely efficient, and therefore must be under the control of people who are familiar with the particular demands of the local environment, physical and social. "Aid" can still be demoralising: there have been occasions even in famines when it was not clear that those who received help suffered less than those who did not. On the other hand, in Ethiopia in 1984, the Mursi obtained only a little free food aid and themselves collected and transported it to their starving people. They have since shouldered the task of achieving economic self-sufficiency with resilience and inventiveness. As with disaster aid, so with emergency help to groups in a new social

in non-traditional activities may affect indigenous societies. Disruption may be minimised by training in collective production and trading with full local participation in planning, implementation and control. On the positive side, community-based marketing may mean control of the local economic process. Whether production is on an individual or collective basis, successful communal marketing can not only increase income but reinforce the identity of the group.

VIII. Recognising women

It has been assumed too often that women will automatically benefit from any improvement in the social and economic position of the group as a whole. In fact it more often happens that changes giving indigenous groups more bargaining power or economic security are achieved at the cost of the women of those groups. Change agents must examine closely the processes governing social change in a given society, and not accept at face value the opinions of atypical informants, probably the leaders of the group and almost certainly male. Women may express satisfaction with the state of affairs, yet their reaction to increased work and gender inequality may be, for instance, voluntary emigration to urban areas, or higher rates of suicide.

A trans-Andean road linking Amuesha territory with Lima has exposed this indigenous group to exploitation of its young women as maids with middle class families of the capital. Indigenous girls are preferred as more hard-working and docile than their urban counterparts. The girls are hired under the pretext that they will receive education as well as lodging, board and some pay. But the Amuesha maids find their duties of cooking, washing, cleaning and child-care for large families onerous and restrictive. Even so more Amuesha girls come to the capital every year, so much so that Amuesha young men find they are seriously short of potential marriage partners. The problem became so severe that the Amuesha Congress produced a play on the dangers to the group's survival of women emigrating to town, taped it and took it around the communities. But the Amuesha girls continued to leave and it became clear that they were prepared to risk the uncertainty of a future in Lima rather than accept the drudgery and subordination of a woman's life in the villages. Unless Amuesha men now take steps to share the burden of subsistence farming, include women in decision making and allow them access to income and secondary education at home, they risk being left alone in their villages.

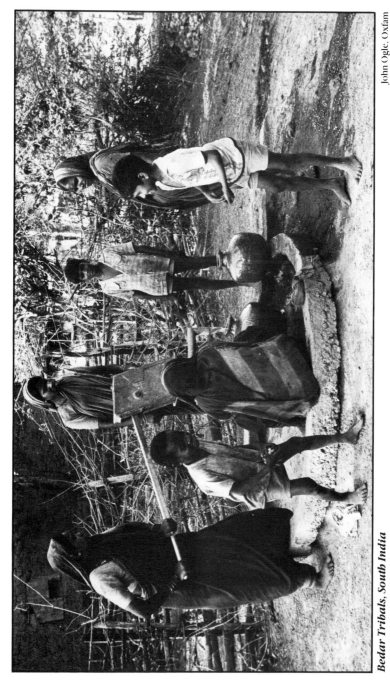

Bedar Tribals, South India

'It has been assumed too often that women will automatically benefit from any improvement in the social and economic position of the group as a whole. In fact it more often happens that changes giving indigenous people more bargaining power or economic security are achieved at the cost of the women of those groups.' (page 45).

John Ogle, Oxfam

Cases of women responding by flight into employment, or of mothers arranging marriages for their daughters in areas where gender roles have changed less painfully, are widely documented.

1. Women fieldworkers

Women fieldworkers are often the first requirement. Even they may find it difficult to obtain information; for men, it may be impossible. It should be the indigenous women who observe and decide what are the effects of change on their work, income, education and role in decision-making. Difficulties may be extreme but, in the end, if power is not won by women, it is not won by the group.

2. Data

An open mind, a listening ear and a creative approach will be of more use than any formal data base, but some themes are often relevant.

i. Residence. Brides who remain with their parents have stronger support than those who join the families of their husbands. Interpretation may vary: the Mundurucu of Brazil had separate residences for males and females, and this was thought by anthropologists to allow considerable female autonomy. The women nevertheless opted to change to residence in the nuclear family common to national society.

ii. Social organisation. What is the structure of households and how large are they? Where extended rather than nuclear families predominate there is greater scope for solidarity between women.

iii. Gender roles. Who does what, in household labour, income generation, subsistence production, decision-making?

iv. Gender relations. Different groups place varying emphasis on the reproductive, productive and sexual functions of males and females. The number of wives (or, more rarely, husbands), age at marriage, dowry or bridewealth, and customs of segregation, divorce and abandonment, may be as important as gender roles in production. Domestic violence may be particularly difficult to detect. Ethnocentrism is a temptation here: in industrial societies, many components of gender relations tend to vary together. Indigenous societies are much more diverse and patterns are much less consistent: women's involvement in income-generation may not correlate with rights to divorce, or inheritance, or political power.

Sexual mores are likely to be under threat from national society and from certain NGOs. Strictly speaking, intervention here is as inadmissible as in other areas of culture. Direct health issues may arise, however: in dependent indigenous societies, venereal diseases contracted from the national society can be a very serious problem.

v. Property rights. Once again, it is easy to fail to appreciate the dissimilarity and complexity of indigenous culture.

In the Northern Territory of Australia, women played little part in Aboriginal claims for their ancestral lands. This proved to be less a function of Aboriginal life than of the assumptions of national society; women now participate with increasing confidence, reinforced by their men. Once again, there was a simple failure by administrators to perceive traditional customs, under which women in this case had a large measure of independent responsibility and authority.

Rights in property and inheritance vary greatly. In the Andes, for instance, bilateral inheritance gives women a voice in the disposal of property and income.

3. Support for women

Birth control services must be an early component of any introduced health care: that is, they must be available if wanted, but never imposed. They must never be seen as a threat to fertility. Health education is commonly the most appropriate beginning, and may usefully include discussion of infertility.

As with other issues, alertness and openness are the first requirement in appreciating what support can usefully be given to women. The dangers are once again diverse. In Kenya, there are groups where only men may plant or fell trees, yet the gathering of fuel for cooking is a wife's responsibility. When the area of accessible bush has been exhausted, acute fuel shortages and domestic conflict may follow. Where the gathering of fuel is onerous, some kind of planting should be considered. "Social forestry" is difficult to achieve, but it may be appropriate to plant fruit and timber trees which can also provide fuel. More efficient stoves may help, and may improve women's respiratory health, but stove projects have often failed: indigenous women must participate in selecting a stove design. Water supplies may be seen as a first priority by the women, who often carry the water; this view is rarely shared by male-dominated local organisations.

It is generally better to improve the position of women by promoting activities they traditionally control rather than by attempting to promote direct conflict with male authority. Subsistence agriculture is often the heaviest burden. This may be alleviated in various ways:

i. by priority support for the subsistence economy.

ii. by seeking to involve men more closely in subsistence farming.

iii. by forms of communal labour.

iv. by ensuring that the best lands and those that are closest to the home are reserved for subsistence production.

v. by making available improved tools for agricultural work and food processing.

vi. by directing agricultural training and credit to women.

vii. by organising so that women have time to attend communal assemblies where they have the right to do so. In Tanzania, women are legally participants, but are usually too busy to be there.

viii. by lessening women's isolation where extended family systems have given way to nuclear families. There is scope for helping women to organise in groups to share the agricultural work or establish communal subsistence plots. Organised groups such as these may go on to exert pressure on male authority, and thus gain the confidence to express views in communal assemblies.

Projects directed specifically to indigenous women can profit whole communities.

In Andhra Pradesh, India, a cyclone created an opportunity for a new beginning. "Integrated Approach to Tribal Development" is a project in South India led by a woman: it operates exclusively for needy tribal women and their families. It began when agriculture was in crisis, being entirely dependent on check dams which had been destroyed in the cyclone. The project is building a new dam, as this is instrumental in gaining credibility with the community and government departments, but it has also promoted bee-keeping, sewing, poultry and kitchen gardening. This is a nascent organisation of women, and its workers meet women development workers from other projects to discuss the problems of tribal women.

Very often, even where women in indigenous society seem traditionally subordinate, the real threat to them comes from national society. All change must be monitored, and every project or intervention evaluated for its effect on women. This is tedious, but the effects are so pervasive that it is the only answer. In many cases only a separate programme can be effective.

4. Income

The need for an income for women is particularly urgent where the family depends on cash for a part of its subsistence, since the men may not regard this as a priority. Income-generating projects for women are most successful where there is a tradition of women's control over their own production. Matrilineal descent among the Shipibo of Peru, for instance, has ensured that Shipibo women benefit from the sale of their crafts: this provides them with an income that complements cash earned by men selling rice. NGO support for a Shipibo co-operative, Maroti Shobo, has improved the economic position of women by promoting their crafts nationally and training women in commercial and administrative skills.

Women in groups that do not have a tradition of control over their own production are less likely to benefit directly from the marketing of their crafts. Men may even exploit women's labour when their production has commercial value. In these cases marketing programmes must establish safeguards for the women and more pains must be taken to ensure both men and women realise that the objective is to secure an income for the women.

5. Education
Educational opportunities for women will not in themselves ensure greater participation in decision-making or strengthen women's bargaining power. But where education is provided to indigenous peoples it is essential that women have equal access, so that lack of knowledge does not act as a further constraint. Appropriate timetables should be arranged for literacy training of adult women who have missed earlier schooling through sex discrimination. Their special needs as agricultural producers may need to be taken into account, so that study does not conflict with subsistence work.

6. Circumcision
Mutilation of the female genitalia is not common among indigenous peoples, but it does occur, and the consequences for health may be severe and life-long. Fieldworkers may find it very difficult to tolerate this practice but should remember that it is deeply embedded in the social structure. Change can only come about when the women of that society have acquired both the consciousness and the power to bring about that change. Nomad women in Mali have protested bitterly that foreign feminists are concerned to stop circumcision rather than to reduce maternal and infant mortality.

7. Senior women
Women's bargaining power may be promoted by identifying and working with those women who enjoy unusual status within groups. Gender inequalities within kinship groups are frequently hierarchical. Women, for instance, who have fulfilled their reproductive roles often enjoy prerogatives not shared by younger women. Matrons such as these may be encouraged to use their greater freedom to help their fellow women to

identify their needs and voice them, though there may be problems where there is conflict between older and younger women.

Particular care needs to be taken of assertions that "women have no need to participate in community assemblies since they may and do exert influence over their husbands' decisions." A similar argument is often used in support of male control of the economy, on the ground that wives may use their "nuisance value" to gain access to income. The tendency of the national society to displace women is so strong that only the most positive action will counter it.

IX. Providing services

1. Introduction
Provision of services for indigenous peoples must mean more than just providing any services instead of none. Services must be culturally acceptable and, as far as possible, self-supporting. Programmes should seek to reinforce rather than replace traditional practices that may be fundamental to self-confidence and self-reliance. Participation must not simply mean receiving services but must imply local control over their design and reception.

2. Health
The needs of indigenous peoples for health services will vary greatly according to their degree of contact with national society. Contact will to a greater or lesser degree have affected the viability of their subsistence economy and the degree of control they exert over their lives in such areas as labour and patterns of settlement. Where subsistence has been severely damaged, health problems may be primarily a function of poverty. Hunger and dirt may be the first things to need attention; a half-starved group with no resources for basic drugs will profit more from food and income than from a health programme. Food may be the best medicine. There is no single model for health services, but there are some guidelines for dealing with the special health needs of indigenous peoples.

i. Respect indigenous practices. All interventions dealing with health need to weigh the advantages of improving health against the possibility of undermining traditional systems. There are basic differences between "scientific" and "traditional" interpretations of sickness. Traditional approaches frequently locate the origins of disease within the social context of the sufferer rather than in infection by germs. Traditional healers may enjoy the trust of the population and will have a great deal of empirical knowledge of the curative properties of many locally available medicinal plants. Health initiatives should at least ensure that the success of traditional healers is not undermined by the introduction of modern health systems; an effort should be made to include them directly in the programme.

Ever since western forms of health care arrived in the jungle region of Peru, traditional Shipibo healers have had to practise their considerable skills surreptitiously. Project Ametra seeks to employ traditional methods of healing and to investigate these in the light of their success. The Ametra team brings Shipibo health workers and university chemists together to examine traditional plant remedies, distinguishing those that are positively beneficial from those that have no apparent effect or are positively harmful. Courses are held in individual communities explaining the value of these traditional cures and a new type of village health worker is emerging; one who receives a balanced training in allopathic medicine from the Ministry doctors and in indigenous techniques from traditional Shipibo healers. The communities are now more interested in health questions, and the health bureaucracy and the non-indigenous population have become aware of traditional medicine.

ii. Stress Primary Health Care. Specialised services are not only impracticable in isolated regions, but will undermine local control and participation through their permanent need for non-indigenous staff. Programmes should aim at basic preventive and curative health care at community level with emphasis on immunisation, control of epidemics, simple curative services, nutrition, mother and child care and sanitation. Village health workers can be trained to cure basic ailments and to encourage preventive measures that require community action, though motivation and reward can be a serious problem.

In certain cases, for example recently contacted groups, a community-based approach will have to give way to a more directed emergency programme. Isolated groups lack immunity to common viral infections such as influenza and mass immunisation and mass treatment may be necessary.

iii. Encourage local control and participation. Because health care is often the most strongly felt need in disrupted societies, there is potential for people to organise around its provision. This may be important in increasing self-confidence and giving rise to organisations. Health committees may involve the population in supervising the village workers and deciding on priorities and may usefully channel the high level of participation generated into other self-help activities.

iv. Plan for finance. Health services will need to be associated with income-generating activities to cover some of the costs. Adequate health care services will involve long-term costs for salaries to village health workers, expenses for volunteer doctors, transport, medical supplies and constant training courses. National health authorities may be unwilling to underwrite the expenses of primary health care for isolated indigenous populations; if a funding agency undertakes this, withdrawal of the agency may result in a severe deterioration of the service. Even basic services will impose a strain on the finances of indigenous organisations, but it is essential to consider the possibilities at an early stage in planning.

There will always be a tension in health projects between the desire of the funding agency to avoid long-term financial commitment and the determination of the group to maintain a service of its own independent of the state system. This is particularly evident where the health service forms the basis of a strong socio-political organisation. Donor agencies should, however, recognise their responsibilities in mounting health care, plan for the long term, and encourage the indigenous group to form representative organisations that can effectively lobby the government for adequate finances for their own services.

3. Education

i. The need. No service is more crucial than formal education. Only new knowledge and skills can enable the group and the individuals within it to plan for their future needs, organise to defend their lands and resources, and manage independent services and commercial enterprises. Most of the training courses for indigenous adults described in this manual assume some knowledge of national languages, institutions and practices; training will therefore be much easier if education has already been given to young indigenous people.

ii. The challenge is to design, implement, supervise and adequately fund systems that meet educational needs without discarding traditional education, knowledge useful for subsistence, cultural vigour and self-confidence. All too often formal education cuts off the pupils from their traditions, undermines distinctive subsistence and cultural practices and creates tensions. The traditional education system must be fully understood before new plans are made. Coordination between the many state, indigenous, and NGO institutions involved in educational policy is also essential.

Among the Mbuti pigmies of Zaire, traditional education seeks to minimise violence and aggression. They grow up to face the world with remarkable confidence, but they have been effectively educated from infancy to avoid conflict — avert it, divert it and, when it erupts despite all precautions, resolve it with a minimum of aggression, physical or verbal. Children are progressively equipped to be a part of a highly integrated, organised community, and to deal with conflict as it arises without the fear that comes from individual isolation and competitiveness. The sense of security and concepts of co-operation and interdependence are promoted from infancy; the child is introduced to all areas of Mbuti life in a complex progression that reinforces values and understanding. To add "formal" education to such sophisticated and successful systems is a daunting challenge.

iii.The programme. Appropriate education for indigenous peoples has the following features:
a. it does not monopolise pupils' time, but relates with understanding to traditional education.
b. it is available locally and does not involve long travel for indigenous students, at least to primary schools. A network of village schools is always preferable to centralised boarding establishments. Local schools ensure that those who want primary education can benefit, without foregoing their traditional education.
c. it is conducted in the language of the group, but provides adequate training in the national language. Bilingual education systems can help to combat official discrimination against minority languages and can encourage their continued use.
d. the curricula are specifically designed for the individual group and are bicultural; that is, aspects of both the national culture and the indigenous culture are studied simultaneously. The bicultural approach to education has proved both effective and supportive of indigenous populations.
e. as far as possible, local indigenous personnel are used as teachers and provided with adequate training, back-up and supervision.

iv. Local control. Since formal education will bring about fundamental changes, there is a need for safeguards to ensure that the process can be directed by the people. Education that locates overall responsibility outside the group will restrict this possibility and involve a surrender of traditional authority. Control of the new educational system must be in the hands of the group. If institutions do not exist, they must be created, starting with education committees at community or village level.

In Peru, non-indigenous Spanish-speaking teachers and a national curriculum have together been a strong force for acculturation. The AIDESEP umbrella organisation of indigenous people has called for a new approach to education, demanding recognition of all indigenous languages in the country and rejecting standardised education. With the University of the Amazon it has set about designing a bilingual education programme, with curricula specifically developed for indigenous cultures and special training for indigenous teachers.

X. The role of the state

The role of the state is of paramount importance; it is the ultimate arbiter of policy and through its regional offices may ensure that decisions taken centrally in favour of indigenous peoples are not just afforded lip-service but are enforced.

1. Favourable state policies

These may include the following:

i. recognition from the state that its society is multi-ethnic and that priorities vary accordingly.

ii. statutory and constitutional guarantees for the rights of indigenous peoples to legal recognition of their lands and resources, to their communal forms of land-holding, to their socio-political and economic organisation, and to their languages.

iii. acknowledgement that indigenous territories may seek quite different futures from the national society.

iv. effective steps to protect indigenous lands from encroachment.

Such policies may involve the enactment of new laws and the overhaul and more generous funding of state institutions responsible for indigenous affairs.

The 1969 Agrarian Reform in Peru afforded legal recognition to the indigenous communities and gave them collective, inalienable rights to their land. This brought the indigenous population of the Andes into the nation's political process and allowed non-indigenous professionals to pursue sizeable land claims on their behalf. Representative organisations were also encouraged, giving the indigenous people a place within the

forum of national politics. The Law of Native Communities of 1974 then gave the indigenous groups of the jungle area the legal foundations for self-management. These groups later adopted the form of organisation described throughout this manual.

The Australian Aboriginal Land Rights (Northern Territory) Act, 1976, is of international significance to indigenous peoples. Some local peoples have secured substantial financial settlements in later negotiations with mining companies. The Gagudju Association was set up to distribute royalties received from the Ranger Uranium project but then became a representative organisation. The royalties have aroused jealousy both within and between groups, and threaten to disrupt gender relations; yet they are also seen as a potential route to autonomy and cultural resurgence. The Gagudju Association has bought a motel within the Kakadu National Park (which means control over alcohol sales over a significant area), thus securing both revenues and employment; it plans to employ a travelling teacher for bush camps, and eventually to establish its own private school. This will enable it to design the curriculum, to avoid having to send children to boarding school for secondary education, and to integrate school hours and terms with Aboriginal needs. Institutions for self-management remain incomplete, and much will depend on immediate developments.

The implication of a favourable state policy is that indigenous peoples have needs that differ from those of national society, and that their interests should not be sacrificed. It does not mean that once they have been awarded land rights indigenous people should be left entirely to their own devices.

v. protecting marginal environments: in planning for indigenous areas, the state is often concerned with delicate ecologies. Scientific opinion is often that indigenous peoples are the best caretakers. In frontier regions particularly, the state may invest in indigenous peoples already occupying the land rather than mount costly colonisation programmes.

vi. constructive state programmes for indigenous peoples will emphasise that resources should be used rationally in a sustainable manner, and turn away from the maximisation of profits from export agriculture. The state needs to differentiate between investments which increase sustainable production and investments which render the existing system non-sustainable.

In Quebec, Canada, after the beaver had been almost wiped out by excessive trapping, the government recognised traditional Cree hunting territories, excluded non-Cree trappers and gave limited cash support while the beaver recovered. Despite two or three centuries of involvement with the international fur trade, the Cree have not been simply passive in the face of external changes, but have sought to set and meet their own objectives. In particular, they seek to retain their ties to the natural environment, their subsistence production, their social structure, their language and their belief systems. The current agreement with the government is for a sufficient guaranteed income for Cree hunters to reduce their dependence on world fur prices, on wages and on welfare benefits. Half the Board which oversees this programme are Cree, and Cree are also formally involved in wildlife management.

XI. The role of non-governmental organisations

NGOs are not necessarily always positive in their impact on indigenous societies, but they do have attributes that may be of value to indigenous peoples, particularly in the field of self-management.

1. Grass-roots contact
NGOs have a commitment to analysing at a local level the real needs of the people with whom they work. This gives them a real opportunity to identify options and devise appropriate action. Their budgetary constraints may be an advantage when they enforce discipline in the selection of projects.

2. Willingness to innovate
In the best cases the unequivocal nature of the NGOs' commitment to the specific group, and its efforts to enable the people to solve their own problems rather than present solutions, may provide inspiration for breakthroughs.

The efforts of the Amuesha people to escape from the domination of the patrons under whom they laboured were not supported by government organisations such as, for example, the Peruvian Agrarian Bank, because the Amuesha were deemed incapable of operating a viable agricultural enterprise. The landowners for whom the Amuesha worked, on the other hand, were always able to take out large loans and use their influence to block any attempts at independence on the part of their workers. It was an NGO that responded to appeals for long-term, low-interest funding of a self-managed agricultural cooperative, independent of the landowners. Though in many senses the project was not a success, it did provide the Amuesha with experience of managing an independent credit programme.

3. The NGO support role

i. Even where indigenous peoples have constitutional guarantees, the state may not always act on their behalf when government policy clashes with their interests. The NGO is not an agent of the state. It may try to ensure that local interests are not subordinated to national strategies.

ii. Where states have suspended guarantees altogether, or make no specific provision for indigenous populations and cultures, the NGO's role will be crucial but much more complex. In extreme cases, the NGO may be able to make international opinion aware of the abuses committed and may support indigenous efforts at gaining a hearing in an international forum with authority acepted by the state. They may be able to demonstrate that long-term economic returns on investment would be higher if policies were more humane, or that land rights now will avoid expensive future litigation. The message must vary with the audience.

iii. NGOs should also capitalise on the things they do best. In the identification of needs, for instance, some groups have clearly defined needs and can agree on areas which require priority; others are more apathetic and are overwhelmed by their situation. Relatively isolated groups are only aware of those possibilities offered by the local power structure; they may have no access to support groups and do not hear of or learn from programmes implemented by and in defence of other groups. Skilled NGO fieldworkers can make all the difference.

PART TWO
ADVICE

APPROPRIATE ACTIVITIES FOR NON-GOVERNMENTAL ORGANISATIONS

I. Introduction

Many NGOs have only fairly recently become aware of the particular needs of indigenous groups. Experience over the past two decades has now convinced NGOs that they merit priority attention; the experience has also shown that the best way to help is not at all obvious.

In most low income countries, sheer numbers render more immediately visible the need of such groups as the rural poor or the urban unemployed. Indigenous people still often occupy inaccessible areas and may be highly mobile. To field staff and officials with no specific background in social anthropology, their culture may seem elusive and their traditions obscure. Their history will tend to be interpreted in the light of the nation's goals and achievements — which in colonised societies are likely be antagonistic to the indigenous population's own goals and achievements.

Moreover, many countries contain not just one homogeneous indigenous people, but a large number of distinct groups, each with its own language and cultural identity. This diversity makes the fieldworker's task more difficult since no single strategy will serve. Working with each group requires considerable specialised knowledge of the individual group in addition to familiarity with the conditions of the country as a whole.

NGOs have nevertheless worked successfully in several areas. In land rights and international solidarity they have often played central roles. Legal aid is a key form of assistance to indigenous people, because legal recognition of their groups and their resources is a precondition of their survival within a nation. In the area of production and income generation, NGOs have come to realise that the economy of indigenous groups is inextricably bound up with social spheres such as kinship, ritual and ideology. They therefore focus assistance on integrated projects which are not purely economic and commercial, but include attention to, for instance, social organisation and legal rights. They also strive to guarantee the subsistence base and support independent marketing operations.

NGOs are particularly active in Primary Health Care, because changes forced upon indigenous people induce dramatic deterioration in health. Less attention has been given to formal education, since NGOs feel responsibility lies primarily with the state. There is still an important role for NGOs in improving indigenous education, and they can usefully support bilingual and bicultural programmes. Discrimination against indigenous people is shown particularly in the provision of services; but the NGO's role as a funding agency is not simply to improve access to these services, but to help indigenous peoples gain increasing control over these vital areas of their lives. To this end it is always important to ensure that all support is accompanied by training.

NGOs prefer to work directly with the representative institutions of indigenous groups or with grass roots associations where they exist. Truly representative institutions, however, are the exception rather than the rule and there is therefore a need for intermediaries. The NGO should assess each case on its merits and should not establish fixed rules about the involvement of outsiders in indigenous communities. The guiding consideration in the role of intermediary support groups is whether the indigenous society is satisfied with their intervention, and whether it serves to foster self-reliance rather than to create dependence.

Self-management may appear the obvious answer to many of the problems of indigenous peoples, but the novelty of the approach is a problem. It also runs against the traditional relations of indigenous peoples with non-indigenous sectors of society and with the state. Self-management is a solution, but not a panacea.

This manual does not seek to cover technical problems, though some are common to many groups. The reader is advised to consult the admirable manuals mentioned at the end of this book.

II. Civil and legal rights

For the majority of groups, the future depends on first securing their fundamental human rights within the national context. The legislation governing the exact status of different indigenous groups varies widely from country to country; some legal codes are systematically punitive, others far more liberal. Certain countries have consistently refused the right of full citizenship to indigenous groups; they are defined as minors in law, under the guardianship of an appointed ministry or agency.

1. The right to citizenship

Where available, citizenship secures legal standing and may make individuals less vulnerable to abuse, but it also imposes national obligations such as voting and military service. Acquisition of "full civil rights" may even be vigorously opposed by indigenous people. In Brazil, the proposed emancipation from tutelage is seen as a way of depriving educated indigenous people of special rights under the law; in Canada, Indians resisted a 1960s policy of abolishing reserves. More often, indigenous peoples without citizenship papers have no legal existence (in the worst cases they may be murdered with impunity), they are subject to harassment and cannot, for instance, travel in any form of public transport or stay in hotels. Those inhabiting border areas face even tighter controls. Help with documentation is often a priority.

Programmes helping people to apply for citizenship seek to streamline the frequently cumbersome bureaucratic process. Legal systems sometimes make provision for local documentation centres, at least for records of birth and issue of birth certificates. Support can be given in establishing village-level registry offices and training indigenous people in their management. In countries such as Peru, where electoral papers serve as identification and proof of citizenship, contacts can be made between indigenous leaders and officials with a view to arranging field visits at which large numbers of people can be enrolled at a time. Such "campaigns" can save individuals months and even years of travel to distant administrative centres in pursuit of full documentation.

2. Keeping watch on legislation

Where indigenous people do not have full civil rights, donor agencies can support groups of professionals which monitor legislation affecting the indigenous population. Laws pertaining to indigenous populations can be amended both for and against their interests. The constitutions of many countries are subject to frequent amendment; it may be possible to secure that an amendment includes guarantees, where they do not already exist.

3. Legal advice

In many countries where the law affecting indigenous peoples is favourable, implementation of the law may be lax owing to powerful local interests. NGOs have funded local intermediary groups which provide professional legal advice to indigenous peoples claiming their rights. The objectives should be to support indigenous leaders in litigation and to provide basic legal training to as many indigenous people as possible, so that they can understand their rights and obligations within the national law. It may be possible to boost confidence with successful test cases that can be publicised nationally, but local groups may not wish to be "used" to establish a principle; equally, they may not wish to trade some immediate gain for a principle. Relevant legal texts may be translated into local languages and reprinted in accessible form. Indigenous contacts with other, similar groups may be widened, in order to make coordinated demands at national level.

III. Land rights

1. Legal title

Legal title to land offers security of tenure. Civil rights are meaningless to indigenous groups unless accompanied by legal provision for the protection of their resources, their communal forms of land-holdings and their political systems. The access of indigenous people to their land base is intimately connected with their legal standing. Many countries accept in principle the rights of indigenous populations to use and possess the lands they occupy, but ownership remains vested in the state and is ultimately at its disposition. Rights of occupancy are highly vulnerable to invasion and indigenous populations generally attempt to gain greater security of land ownership through tenure by title. Mineral rights and the right to protest about innovations such as dams or pipelines may also be involved. During negotiations for title, there is a danger of extinction of aboriginal rights of settlement; this must be given close legal attention.

Such rights need also to be secured locally. In the Upper Urubamba Valley,Peru, Machiguenga communities followed the achievement of land rights by planting the new boundaries with commercial tree and other crops, making them immediately identifiable.

2. Consultation

Fieldworkers must always find out how the group in question wishes to claim recognition of its territory — whether in the name of the individual community, or of groups of communities or of the entire ethnic group. The tendency of Latin American states, for instance, is to regard the community as the maximum unit for recognition of land claims. While not satisfying indigenous land needs to the fullest extent this is certainly preferable to breaking up territories into smallholdings. NGO policy should be to support efforts to secure communal land titles, where desired, on the understanding that the programme extends to all the communities of a given area. The vesting of legal rights in individuals rather than communities is a serious threat to indigenous peoples, and should be accepted only in the last resort when a group are virtually landless and homeless.

Where land is vested in the community, modes of recruitment to the community must be identified and circumscribed in such a way as to safeguard traditional flexibility while preventing abuse by outsiders. Problems of definition have been severe in Australia, where the national judiciary have had some difficulty with concepts of "the tracks of the ancestors", or "the dreaming".

REGISTERED SACRED SITE

THIS PLACE IS A SACRED SITE
FOR THE AYIPARINYA CATERPILLAR
DREAMING.
PLEASE HELP US TO PROTECT IT.

ENTRY BY MOTOR VEHICLE
IS PROHIBITED.

Penalty for damage or desecration
of the area

$2000

or imprisonment for 12 months or both.

ABORIGINAL SACRED SITES AUTHORITY
AT REQUEST OF ABORIGINAL CUSTODIANS

Aboriginal People, Australia   Survival International

*'Fieldworkers must always find out how the group in question wishes to claim
recognition of its territory — whether in the name of the individual community, or of
groups of communities or of the entire ethnic group.'* (page 64).

3. Isolated groups

This last process generally applies to those groups which are in permanent contact with national society and have acquired some familiarity with the nation's forms of land ownership and settlement. The problem is far more complex for isolated groups who have relatively little contact with society, such as the Waorani of Ecuador and the Yanomami of Brazil and Venezuela. As wide-ranging hunters, gatherers and gardeners, extensive territories are crucial to survival. Yet the attempts to secure legal recognition of entire territories often gives rise to an insurmountable conflict of interests between governments and indigenous peoples. Very large areas are often involved and these may be regarded by governments, and by the dominant sectors of society they represent, as out of all proportion to the size of the indigenous population.

The reluctance of governments to recognise corporate ownership of territories can be mitigated in countries with community systems by demarcating continuous boundaries. When these are associated with buffer zones such as national parks or conservation areas which the people can use for traditional resource management, an approximation to the entire original territory can be achieved. Where no provision for communal landholding exists, support for national and international solidarity campaigns can inspire special legislation to create indigenous territories.

4. Land titling programmes

These can be implemented by specialist NGOs. Land titling is generally the responsibility of the ministry or other government institution responsible for indigenous affairs. Local state institutions, however, are frequently understaffed, and rarely have the resources, the motivation or even the technical capacity to undertake the reconnaissance, cadaster and demarcation of isolated areas. NGOs have filled this gap by supporting independent groups of professionals which have made prior agreements with the government that they will undertake the fieldwork on behalf of the indigenous people. The process differs according to the legal system but may involve:

i. consultations with the people and their representative institutions.

ii. contracts both from the state and the indigenous people.

iii. social surveys of indigenous territories, including accurate census data and anthropological reports.

iv. definition of community membership (see consultation, above).

v. legal negotiations concerning recognition of the communities to be titled.

vi. resolution of conflicting claims to the land by settlers or contractors.

vii. topographical surveys with technical reports on natural resources and potential land use.

viii. drafts of scale plans to support the petition and their approval by the local government bureaucracy.

ix. presentation of the documentation to the ministry for approval.

x. registration of the land titles in public records offices.

As soon as the Peruvian Law of Native Communities was enacted in 1974 it was obvious to both the indigenous peoples and their supporters that this was an instrument of great potential value. Intermediary groups rapidly formed teams of specialists including anthropologists, lawyers, topographers and soil scientists to ensure that the indigenous people benefited to the full from the dispositions governing the extension and type of terrain to be ceded under title. NGO support covered the costs of air and river transport for these teams, their salaries, insurance (necessary for the isolated areas they worked in for many months) and expenses related to the protracted legal negotiations. The process was arduous, bureaucratic and fraught with conflict. Even with the considerable expertise of the protagonists, the process could be drawn out over two or three years and fresh obstacles were found at every stage of the titling campaign. Political considerations governed the final approval of the land titles and from 1976 to 1979 a shift in priorities froze the programme. Even so, by 1985 more than 1000 indigenous communities had been recognised and over 600 inalienable land titles had received ministerial signature — largely as a result of the efforts of intermediary organisations. In just over a decade the combination of political will at central government level, Indian demands and NGO grass-roots know-how had radically transformed the legal standing of the Peruvian lowland Indian.

5. How much land?

Any programme entering into issues of land titling must consider problems of land sufficiency and must be able to justify ecologically, economically and socially, the amounts of land demarcated. For hunters and gatherers, pastoral nomads and shifting cultivators, the area required for sustained subsistence may be very large; accurate surveys of traditional practices are essential to justify the upper limits. Many countries have an arbitrary ceiling on the amount of land that can be titled. Additional factors to take into account are:

i. forecast population increases.

ii. special legal requirements, for instance for seasonally flooded alluvial lands. These are frequently under strong pressure from incoming settlers and may need to be titled separately.

iii. nomads may share land by using it at different times. In these and other cases, indigenous groups may be in conflict, and this makes finding a solution difficult. Traditional cattle raiding in East Africa is not readily "solved" by legislation.

6. Indigenous participation

Demarcation of lands must be undertaken closely with the peoples involved. Community members can:

i. define community membership, where relevant.

ii. identify their territorial limits.

iii. clear boundaries, maintain them and place markers.

iv. learn the process by which titles are gained.

v. establish relationships with local state officials.

This experience is vital for the defence of boundaries and at a later stage it might be possible for the communities to claim increases in their titled territories.

7. State participation

It is equally important that the local agrarian or other relevant authorities are not by-passed but are closely involved in the process. The departure of an outside titling team will leave a vacuum if the local authorities and the communities have not established relations of mutual confidence. When NGOs have supported intermediary groups whose field methodology is based on strengthening these contacts, they would discourage interventions that try to take over the role of official agencies. Cooperation can make the staff of official agencies more aware of the problems of indigenous people. Fieldworkers who are professionally engaged in mediating between indigenous peoples and the state can become hostile and disparaging about state officials. This may be quite unfair, given the relative scale of resources and problems, and is in any event counter-productive.

8. Follow up

Land titles are not sufficient. In the early years of a land reform law, or special legislation for indigenous peoples, there is a temptation for support groups to rush land titling programmes and shelve other activities. But people still need to be helped to defend their titled lands, to participate in the economy as far as they wish and to adjust their socio-political and economic structure to fit the new situation.

IV. Subsistence

The reader is reminded that the Oxfam Field Directors' Handbook, recommended in Part Three, provides much practical advice on development work. The present manual concentrates on problems specific to indigenous groups.

1. Total loss of lands

The priority should always be to re-establish a land base, preferably in the traditional territory. Shortages of food may be severe where the land base has been reduced through invasion or environmental degradation, or where indigenous peoples have been resettled. Cultivators may be unable to produce adequate staples rich in carbohydrate. Where land has been lost, efforts can be made to relocate the group, possibly even by purchasing new lands on their behalf. Where resettlement is unavoidable, members of the group should be enabled to open gardens in the resettlement area before the arrival of the main population so that fast-growing varieties of the staple can be planted. Food aid should only be a last resort as dependence can be created very quickly.

2. Regreening programmes

These may restore eroded land, but require great motivation.

On Sabu Island, Nusa Tenggara Timur, Indonesia, subsistence is being undermined by loss of tree cover, soil erosion and perennial drought. Shifting cultivation gave way to settled agriculture without protection for trees; cattle and other domestic animals roam at will, preventing regeneration. A voluntary organisation has village volunteers and a small paid staff. Forty villages are involved in tree planting, both a leguminous fodder tree and fruit and nut trees; the village schools cultivate small tree nurseries in addition to their school gardens. Traditionally, animals are often tied in the rainy season, but released to forage in the dry. Some villages have instituted livestock control; in Ledeana, owners of stray animals are fined, and if the fine is not paid, the animal is slaughtered. This is not popular with neighbouring villages. Community participation in decision-making is insufficient, and is possibly threatened by NGO funds which are allowing a rapid switch to salaries and technical expertise, but the programme has great promise.

3. Protein for cultivators

Rather than total land loss, indigenous people more frequently find their land base restricted to various degrees. The strongest nutritional need felt by cultivators may then be for protein: the starch they can still grow, but once pressure on land reduces crop diversity and availability of fish and game, protein becomes a problem. There has been little research into supplementing protein for indigenous groups because research priorities have rarely been set with their demands in mind. Initiatives in this field should resist any proposal to transform existing systems on the assumption that they are no longer viable. Converting forest to pasture to breed cattle, for instance, is more likely to create hunger than to supply a population's needs for meat, yet in Latin America it is a common official choice.

A simple technology can often restore a people's access to protein without undermining the traditional system. The new technology can be incorporated within traditional horticultural practices. NGOs have supported programmes that seek to remedy the protein shortage by encouraging greater use of traditional bean crops, introducing new legumes, promoting indigenous small livestock and improving fishing tools. Projects aimed at boosting subsistence for indigenous populations have often ignored the contribution of food that can be gathered from the forest, greatly to the detriment of indigenous diets. The habitats of insects and larvae can be protected. Garden hunting is often traditional with forest peoples: game animals are allowed to raid gardens and then culled. Such activities are often abandoned by indigenous groups in the face of the scorn of national society. Settlers on the Transamazon highway suffered from protein deficiency in the midst of plenty through their disdain for local game and invertebrates.

Quick results can be achieved against protein deficiency by diffusing poultry widely and attending to their veterinary needs. Technicians should beware of introducing exotic breeds since these frequently succumb to disease. Stocks for distribution should be built up using local breeds, although limited cross-breeding can boost egg and meat production without endangering immunity. Systems need to be found that rely little on purchased inputs. Ambitious collective poultry farms, for instance, should be discouraged — they rarely work. Protein deficiencies are best remedied by decentralised family unit production. In village settings, where the total poultry population is high, constant veterinary care will be essential.

Outside South-East Asia, many collective fish breeding projects have failed but if they inspire individuals to maintain family ponds the future possibility of take-up on a wider scale remains.

4. Pastoral nomads

Here the problem is rather to restore pastoralism and, in the last resort, to supplement this with some cropping possibilities. Pastoral subsistence is at present often severely threatened, by drought, desertification, cattle raiding and civil war. The vast majority of official programmes for pastoralists have been technical, economic and social failures, but pastoralism itself is a sophisticated adaptation.

A group of Afar pastoralists in the valley area bordering the Awash National Park, Ethiopia, lost their livestock in a drought. They took to farming with great ingenuity and no little enthusiasm, hiring advice from landless sharecroppers from the southern Sudan. The Afar are squeezed by the neighbouring Issa, who seem more successful at controlling access to pasture, and by the state, seeking to increase its access to pasture and irrigable lands. This group feel they have lost their status with their animals; also, their fields are raided by their nomadic brethren. An NGO has given a grant to help the Afar group to rebuild livestock capital; then they will be able to decide whether they wish to be agriculturalists, agro-pastoralists or nomads, and to give the Sudanese sharecroppers some capital in livestock against the day when the Afar no longer need them to help farm.

The improvement of livestock unfortunately calls for co-ordinated action in land and water rights, water development, veterinary services, animal husbandry, range management, livestock marketing and community development. It is often very difficult to obtain co-ordination at the local level. Probably the most effective single intervention for pastoral nomads has been water development, but this can also be very destructive. It may lead to overgrazing and human and animal disease, or local construction of water supplies may actually accelerate the transition to individual land holding. Nevertheless, water development is essential for range management. In Africa, browse resources are very important and have consistently been underestimated by outsiders; research has tended to focus on grass resources. Water harvesting has not been successful with nomads.

There are very few "technical packages" for improved livestock production which yield results demonstrably superior to pastoralists' own practices. Outside breeds often perform poorly so that breed improvement is not an easy option. Camels and milking goats are being introduced to ex-cattle pastoralists in areas subject to increasing drought or with ample

Nigel Clarke, Oxfam

Beja Boy, Sudan
'The improvement of livestock... calls for co-ordinated action in land and water rights; water development; veterinary services; animal husbandry; range management; livestock marketing and community development.' (page 71).

browse: they can be a tremendous advantage to nomads who must live on milk for extended periods. Both are browsers and so productive for a longer time in the dry season.

5. Indirect action
Indigenous subsistence may be improved by investment which reduces pressure upon the group.

The Tan Long Reservoir in Vietnam has received NGO support specifically because it will restore livelihood to the local Muong and Kinh minorities. Agriculture is at present limited by availability of water: the dam will make dry season irrigation possible, and will expand the area irrigated in the monsoon. The present cultivated area does not meet the food needs of the local population, so that trees are felled for sale and for crops. This threatens the livelihood of the Muongs, who depend on the forests and fallow to graze their livestock, though they also participate in the agriculture. Much of Thanh Hoa province is severely deforested, eroded and susceptible to drought; it is hoped that a secure food supply will permit reforestation.

6. Conclusion
A group that enjoys unimpaired subsistence, or has taken steps to restore subsistence viability, can turn its attention to income-raising and commercial activities. As long as the subsistence base is assured, there is less risk to the people in devoting measured proportions of their lands and time to raising income by agriculture.

V. Raising income
1. Introduction
Activities related to raising income in indigenous societies are important on a number of counts:
i. to satisfy individual needs for commodities.
ii. to provide communal income for services.
iii. to legitimise land titles where surplus agricultural production is seen as the only rational use of land.

Introducing indigenous peoples to commercial activities requires a cautious approach. The need for cash income can easily come to dominate projects. Where possible, income-raising programmes should be integral and include training in such areas as social organisation, ecology, technology, accountancy and marketing.

Very often the indigenous group is already in receipt of income, on unfavourable terms. Schemes to improve their position often integrate several projects.

In Koraput, Orissa, India, village committees manage all the work for indigenous development; their organisation seeks to check the monopoly business of moneylenders, to increase wages and to improve crop prices. This has arisen out of an emergency. Severe flooding in the Vamsadhana River valley attracted an NGO to initiate operational flood rehabilitation. The team stayed on to start a social action project after the relief phase; it built up the strength of the village committees and organised common funds for grain storage and agricultural credit. The indigenous people are now taking an interest in prices, weights and measures, wage rates etc; in thirteen villages, people have stopped taking loans from moneylenders and are using common funds or approaching the banks. In some villages, women are participating in common issues such as minimum wage, land problems etc. The range of activities is very wide, from cooperation with the government in building schools to the planting of fruit trees and adult education.

2. Export commodities

Export crops are widely cultivated by indigenous peoples. The crops most compatible with subsistence economies will be those that have relatively low labour requirements, command reasonable gains at world market prices, and have a high per kilo value and are thus easier to transport. Groups in the high forest regions of the Amazon, for instance, have incorporated coffee and cocoa into their traditional gardens. They have found that relatively small amounts of land can yield higher incomes than would be gained by selling labour or by cultivating food crops required on the national market (see below). Similar strategies have been common in South-East Asia over a longer period: success has tended to depend on the crop and its world market characteristics. Programmes supporting the introduction of high value tree crops such as coffee and cocoa should:

i. avoid establishing large, monocropped plantations and capital-intensive techniques.

ii. introduce low-input technology such as pruning, disease-resistant seed and locally available fertilisation.

iii. encourage ecologically sound practices such as leguminous shade trees. These reduce yield but benefit the soil by fixing nitrogen and preventing erosion.

iv. diversify production as a safeguard against fluctuating world market prices. Forms of agroforestry, in which trees, crops and livestock complement each other, may echo the diversity and complexity of traditional strategies.

Recommending that indigenous peoples become involved in producing export crops may appear paradoxical when export crops often threaten subsistence. This is one example where the needs of particular indigenous peoples can be at variance with global trends.

3. Food crops

The sale of food crops on the national market is often recommended as an income-generating strategy for peasant societies because, unlike commodities, the food crops can be consumed if they cannot be sold for any reason. But fieldworkers should beware of encouraging indigenous farmers to sell their own food crops or plant new food crops for sale.

i. Indigenous farmers may be tempted (or may need) to sell too large a proportion of their staple crop and then go hungry.

ii. Food crops are often poor earners; this is usually compounded in the case of indigenous groups by their distance from markets. There are wide seasonal fluctuations in the prices of staples, and prices are often artificially lowered by national food-importing policies. Small-scale food producers as a whole generally have only limited bargaining power in the national society.

iii. Bulky food crops are hard to transport and store, are labour-intensive, and take out large areas from subsistence production if they are cultivated on a scale that earns a reasonable income.

Food production may nevertheless be the only income-raising possibility. In these cases indigenous farmers will need training in new agricultural approaches. Introducing this type of technology to indigenous groups runs counter to the recommendations made above to preserve traditional agricultural systems and avoid radical changes in production patterns. Indigenous groups forced by circumstances to adapt farming systems need professional support that is aware of developments in low input agricultural and pastoral technology.

4. Cattle

In Latin America, cattle are one of the least appropriate yet most common means of generating economic surplus for indigenous communities in forest regions. They rarely serve subsistence needs since their meat is not consumed, their milk is not available, and they are low earners in comparison with alternative uses of the same amount of land. However, cattle are frequently seen as a prestigious asset and a hedge against financial emergencies, such as the need for emergency medical treatment. On occasion, cattle serve as a means of defending lands subject to encroachment. It may for instance be possible to combat encroachment on indigenous territories by establishing pastures along stress lines such as roads. In Ecuador, for instance, the Quichua of the Napo have responded to the need for raising income and protecting lands by using communal work to establish pastures on either side of the road penetrating their territory. This is a variation of the agricultural "living frontier" programme of the Machiguenga of Peru.

In Gujarat, India, producers' dairying cooperatives have reached thousands of the very poor. Tribal people in the forests can feed their buffaloes on collected fodder. Buffaloes need a carefully balanced diet including green fodder, readily available in the forest and brought in by bullock cart. By bringing the fodder to the buffalo, the natural regeneration of the forest is protected and the buffalo does not waste energy which it could otherwise use in milk production. Under the state Tribal Sub-Plan, groups of farmers can get a 50 per cent subsidy for purchasing up to two buffaloes; the rest of the price is available from banks at a subsidized rate, subject to a small deposit. This deposit is critical, and it is here that NGOs have been able to help, spreading the benefits of the expanding dairy business beyond the rich coastal plain of Gujarat to the indigenous people of the interior. One intermediary group collected the milk by jeep for a year to convince the dairy that the villages would provide reliable supplies of milk; the dairy then established a new truck route. Buffalo milk offers an alternative or additional source of income to migrant casual labour, while the experience of group organisation may be even more important.

5. Alternative income-generating activities
All should be tested against the guidelines of benefit, dependence and impact on subsistence production.

i. Natural resources. Brazil nuts, wild rubber or minerals, for instance, when they occur in indigenous territories, can provide an income with minimal ecological disruption, but will be destructive unless there is legal support to ensure that these resources and access to them remain firmly under the control of the indigenous people. "Windfall" gains are also a severe threat, arising, for example, when enlightened legislation leads to the payment of royalties to indigenous groups by mining corporations. Without organisation, the money can do more harm than good, leading to divisions in the society; even in an organised group, the surplus funds suddenly available, usually only to the men, can be difficult to manage, disrupt gender relations, and leave the group open to exploitation. Peoples in Canada and Australia have been much engaged in seeking answers to this potentially very serious problem.

ii. Timber. Timber is a resource rarely exploited to the benefit of indigenous people. The pressures to treat timber as a one-off product are generally strong. NGOs can contribute by giving access to technical knowledge in forest management which can make this valuable source of income renewable and of long-term benefit to the people.

iii. Social forestry. This is often not an easy option, but in India, the forest-dwelling tribal peoples of Sagrun, Rajasthan, have developed a good mix of fruit, fodder, timber and bamboo. They depend on the forest for their livelihood and have been impoverished by its contraction; communal planting restores some command over their lives.

iv. Crafts. Crafts can partly satisfy the need for income of groups with a distinctive material culture. They can provide an income to both men and women; their production requires no training; and they use resources available locally. NGOs which support income generation through commercial production of crafts will need to confront the marketing constraints that tend to reduce income to producers.

The difficulties of marketing indigenous crafts should not be underestimated. The market is specialised; demand for individual articles is highly volatile; quality tends to fall as production increases; crafts are often delicate and require special packaging and care; because exotic crafts are highly prized indigenous peoples rarely control marketing. They depend on middlemen.

Commercial and tourist crafts are usually somewhat modified for purposes of sale. There will be pressures for this from within the culture where traditional art is sacred; in Central Australia, for instance, the Aranda used not to sell their churingas or even show them to outsiders.

Market pressures will also affect design: souvenirs must be cheap, portable, attractive and dustable! Marketing of crafts cannot be considered a mere afterthought to broader commercial enterprises. It requires specialised fieldworkers who assess the sales potential of the crafts of a given group, research production techniques, ensure quality does not suffer from commercialisation, promote the crafts on the market and train indigenous personnel to manage marketing, often in craft cooperatives. (See also Part One, Section 3, IV, 2.)

These activities require specialised centres at local and national level. Maroti Shobo, for example, is an NGO-sponsored centre that markets the highly commercial crafts of the Shipibo Indians of Peru, providing management training and encouraging organisational, agricultural and commercial enterprises in the 100 communities it serves. In Peru many such centres in the coastal, Andean and forest regions are represented nationally by the Antisuyo Marketing Centre based in Lima. Antisuyo seeks solid international markets for the products of its affiliates; it arranges training for local co-operatives and attempts to promote their interests nationally.

VI. Credit

1. Introduction

Indigenous peoples who have no access to commercial or state credit may have no other sources, or they may be able to turn to the traditional patron, or to apply to an NGO for support. The system of advancing goods in return for indigenous labour has so distorted the life of many indigenous groups that they no longer even aspire to independence. NGO programmes that seek to offset the evident exploitation of such a system should not, except in an emergency, go to the other extreme of simply providing free credit — that is, gifts. Free credit commonly creates another form of dependence, but may be unavoidable in, for instance, reconstruction after disaster. Normally the aim of NGO intervention will be to enable the indigenous group to make successful use of commercial and state credit; NGO credit has very specific uses. Appropriate credit schemes must bear some relationship to the understanding of the people, and can even be inspired by existing systems.

The Peruvian share system of acquiring cattle clearly functions to the disadvantage of the receiver. A rancher supplies his labourer with a cow in calf which the labourer will look after on his own pasture. In due course he will return the original cow and half the offspring. A debt relationship is established at the expense of the labourer, who carries all the responsibility of the animals. The rancher avoids the cost of maintaining pasture and gains an effort-free return on his investment. Brazil and Ecuador have similar patterns.

A variation on this credit form has been successfully applied by many NGOs. Under the more benign "by halves" system, the client keeps the original animal and merely passes on one of the offspring. Credit systems based on this form of sharing can rapidly spread livestock through communities that desire them, without creating new forms of dependence.

In Niger, the Wodaabe have a tradition of mutual help and solidarity through the "animal of friendship". The lender temporarily renounces all rights over the animal, for milk and offspring, but reclaims it after the second or third calf. The tradition does not lead to dependence and is partly an insurance mechanism against risk as animals are distributed in different ecological zones. With the help of an intermediary, an NGO was able to buy animals on the markets and lend them as animals of friendship to reconstitute herds after drought and famine. Almost all the animals were returned to the project according to the tradition, but it was not possible to extend the practice to groups without the tradition. In Mali, the same NGO lent money for the reconstitution of herds, but felt that the need for cash repayment delayed reconstitution.

2. Other forms of NGO credit

i. Working capital. Working capital for commercial enterprises may be best given as a loan rather than a grant, though the specific circumstances must dictate what action is taken (see Oxfam's Manual of Credit and Savings). The cost of a grant will often be offset against the work the community does itself, putting in place and maintaining infrastructure.

ii. Revolving loan funds. These can be particularly effective in marketing operations when a centre with its own working capital wishes to respond to the needs of individual communities for local community-based stores. There is likely to be competition for available credit and communities who receive the loan will not wish to prejudice their standing by default. Many such funds within indigenous communities have also been very successful.

iii. Direct credit. Credit given directly to individuals within indigenous groups should normally not be encouraged, nor should individual communities be favoured by an NGO. Credit should always be channelled through representative institutions, thus strengthening management in the group's leadership. The objective should always be for the group to have the skills and confidence to draw credit on good terms from national society.

The Disha Trust, in Gujarat, India, seeks to promote and serve small village groups. Government programmes have had little effect on the lives of the very poor, such as the tribal peoples. Disha sees the development of confidence and independence as all-important: the groups take their own decisions about activities, and only then apply to Disha for funding. Groups have been funded for milk cooperatives, a bamboo workers' cooperative, irrigation facilities, administrative costs, and the costs of applying for government or bank loans. The credit is a means to an end, to promote organisation. The small village groups enforce fair wages, run adult education classes, re-afforestation and agricultural schemes and discuss complaints concerning forest, land, police etc. Disha helps them to avail themselves of government schemes. The credit does have a role in income generation, but its role is primarily in the development of organisation.

VII. Training

1. Introduction
The greatest contribution NGOs can make to indigenous wellbeing lies in training the people to manage their own programmes. Too often, through lack of personnel or time, interventions are restricted to providing funds or technology when the real need is for patient and well thought-out grounding in their use.

In the Mountain Province of Luzon, the Philippines, DATC, an agency staffed almost entirely by people from local tribal communities, trains para-professionals and community volunteers. It has developed one of the most innovative approaches in the world to functional literacy. It links the development of community organisation to the establishment of functional literacy programmes in each village and to the implementation of agricultural programmes. The classes discuss problems and take up income generating projects, particularly in agricultural production and marketing. Even though the staff are indigenous, they seek to train local people as trainers, so that DATC can withdraw from direct involvement and serve in a consultancy capacity. They also run refresher courses. Wherever possible, training is community-based.

2. Agricultural extension

i. Indigenous farming systems. To understand just what technology is required and will be acceptable means first learning the indigenous farming system. In many cases the indigenous people themselves will be aware of the kinds of changes they most need, but may not express them unless they have confidence in the planners. This is because experience has taught them that agricultural technicians have fixed ideas of their own and generally have a poor opinion of customary systems. Though time-consuming, effort spent on establishing relations of trust and enabling the people to express their own ideas will not be wasted, since the task of introducing a technology that does not respond to a real need will encounter every kind of difficulty later in the programme.

ii. Identifying the technology. Changes with a chance of taking root will tend to be those that:

a. can be easily explained and show quick results;

b. fit into the existing subsistence system without upsetting traditional social relations;

c. use local resources as far as possible.

Training must not be restricted to men: efforts must be made to locate opportunities for women relevant to their roles in the farming system.

iii. Delivering the technology. When the new technology is identified, delivery and propagation are crucial. Village participation on a broad level, including men and women, is essential to achieve wide adoption of new technology. This will avoid the inequalities that partial acceptance can entail. Methods of training will be most effective when they include traditional systems such as collective labour.

Demonstration plots established communally have the advantage of including a large sector of the population in the training process, giving individuals the opportunity to practise the new technology, discuss it and watch the results before adopting it in their own fields or gardens.

Para-vets or "barefoot vets" have been trained among the Mundari of Equatoria, South Sudan. In Equatoria, there is an almost total lack of veterinary staff, drugs and equipment; epidemics are a regular feature. Civil war and cattle raiding have forced the Mundari to concentrate their herds, facilitating the rapid spread of disease. A local self-help group developed the project. Men who were skilled with cattle were selected by chiefs for training, which was mainly in Juba because of the insecurity of the countryside; prevention and vaccination were emphasised. The para-vets proved much more successful in vaccination than the ministry personnel,

Mundari People, Sudan

Jon Bennett, Oxfam

'The para-vets proved much more successful in vaccination than the ministry personnel, partly because of personal contacts and partly because they were willing to spend the night in cattle camps.' (page 81).

partly because of personal contacts, partly because they were willing to spend the night in cattle camps. In the early morning large numbers of cattle are not only concentrated but lying down and easily vaccinated. The self-help group had acquired cold-chain facilities and initial funding from an NGO; a revolving fund was set up, with prices charged slightly above cost to pay the para-vets. Payment has been acceptable, possibly because losses of stock are so costly. Most problems have arisen from the civil war, which creates difficulties in supervising the para-vets and in maintaining supplies of drugs and vaccines.

iv. Selecting extensionists. Long-term improvements in agriculture will require indigenous personnel to be trained as extensionists, or agricultural teachers. These should be selected from those people that have shown the most motivation to work voluntarily and have inspired the most enthusiasm in their communities. Further selection can then be made of programme leaders who will be reponsible for the project after the departure of the fieldworkers.

v. Training extensionists. Indigenous extensionists are only as good as the back-up they receive, and training must go hand in hand with practical support to the extensionists and the communities they serve. The Mundari depend on their supplies of drugs and vaccines, and the maintenance of the cold-chain. Local training courses are always preferable to long, semi-professional study in distant institutions that may have no knowledge of the areas the students come from. Courses should be carefully planned around the specific technology or crop to be introduced. Short, specific courses enlivened by visual aids, role play, local methods of communication and field visits should be spread through the year in time with the agricultural calendar.

vi. Programme leaders. Agricultural projects are frequently over-ambitious in their training objectives, particularly those that depend on a trained extensionist or village level worker in each of a large number of communities. Unlike health services, which can justify training of workers on this scale, agricultural extension services receive little state support and so are more difficult to maintain in the long run. Morale tends to be low among unpaid extensionists with a heavy work load. An alternative is the intensive training of a small, mobile team of full-time programme leaders. During the course of the project fieldworkers transfer to the team the necessary technical, administrative, financial and planning skills to back up the volunteer extensionists; the team implements its own training programme in the communities. Where effective inter-community organisations exist, these programme leaders often form part of the organisation as a production committee.

The CEDIA intermediary group, which supports seven Machiguenga communities in the high forest region of Peru against settler incursions, places training firmly at the centre of its land defence programme. Boundary strips established by communal labour need agricultural support and training in surveying boundary lines, establishing nurseries, transplanting seedlings and caring for the young trees. Courses, in which video techniques feature strongly, are held on a rotating basis among the seven communities, with the attendance of five members from each visiting community and a much larger participation of the host community. As well as assuring wide diffusion of the technology, this approach to training has had the effect of bringing together members of previously isolated villages. Cooperation over land defence and agricultural training is laying the foundations of a Machiguenga organisation.

3. Training in marketing
Training in marketing skills needs to allow for all those factors that have made indigenous self-run marketing operations so easy to launch and yet so hard to continue. There are three principal limitations.

i. Technical. Problems may arise in such areas as literacy, numeracy, accountancy and (where motorised transport is involved) mechanics.

ii. Administrative. Areas such as planning, attention to the details of the business, taking into account the effects of inflation in pricing and budgetting etc.

iii. Social. Problems may include dissension, lack of participation, dishonesty and bad debts; "social" limitations like these may be the most fundamental.

Broad-based practical training to overcome these limitations is best achieved through projects that allow people to identify the administrators of the marketing operation and hold them accountable. Training should not be limited to passing on skills just to the elected representatives; they must also be made available to the people represented. Both assemblies and administrators may need to learn ways of making and receiving constructive criticism, participating creatively in the enterprise and accepting that failures can give useful experience.

Courses in literacy, numeracy, accountancy and simple forms of co-operative organisation can also be directed towards the population at large or its communal representatives, to ensure new skills are not restricted to a privileged few. Where many communities are involved in marketing operations, committees can be formed at local level with provision for training around the operation of village stores.

Simple pre-cooperative structures rather than sophisticated institutions will enable people to understand and organise marketing operations. It is far easier to upgrade a marketing operation that is successful than to rebuild one that has failed because it was institutionally inappropriate.

By 1985 the Aguaruna and Huambisa Council in Peru administered a system providing for the commercial needs of a hundred indigenous communities through nine warehouses which sell by wholesale to 67 village markets. Annual production handled by the Aguaruna commercial system amounts to 500 tons of cocoa beans, 18 kilos of gold, 352 tons of rice and 150 tons of beans. Training for this still-growing enterprise involved designing an appropriate structure with the Aguaruna and ensuring a high level of accountability at all levels of financial management. By tradition astute traders, the Aguaruna were able to acquire many of the basic skills of a viable business simply through practice. The intermediary group advising on the commercial operation provided a training model, based on accountancy, business administration and organisation, to support indigenous aspirations for self-management. Business connected with the productive and commercial process has become an important topic of the Aguaruna and Huambisa village assemblies, which are lively, lengthy and often highly critical of elected officials.

VIII. Health

Again, excellent manuals on Primary Health Care exist (see Background Reading, p.119), but there are difficulties specific to indigenous peoples.

1. Conflict

The intervention may be viewed quite differently by the NGO and the indigenous population. While the NGO's aim is to encourage a basic system emphasising low costs, simple curative treatment, preventive measures and training of village health workers, the indigenous people or their representative institutions may initially expect well-stocked pharmacies and a curative approach applied by non-indigenous professionals.

It is essential for this to be considered at the planning stage, or the intervention will be plagued by misunderstandings. Too strict an interpretation of Primary Health Care principles may undermine the programme's credibility. The problem is to meet needs without allowing costs, infrastructure or use of modern curative practices to create dependence. There is clearly a need from the start for wide discussions between the NGO and the representative institutions of the group. Yet the institutions of the people may not be sufficiently broad-based to represent priority groups within the society. New committees may be needed for the design, implementation and administration of the programme.

2. Community diagnosis

One method of involving people in the aims and scope of the project is by drawing the community into the assessment of the extent of ill-health, the definition of priorities and the plans to combat disease. The input of medical advisers will be necessary to help estimate the incidence of disease and offer insights into causes that are beyond the experience of the people. People are often aware that health conditions are deteriorating, but they are usually unable to explain the reasons in terms understandable to practitioners of western medicine. Similarly, health staff will encounter difficulties in putting across relationships which may seem basic to them, such as that between hygiene and diarrhoea. When carried out jointly by the people and the medical personnel the community diagnosis presents an opportunity for all involved to explore differences in attitudes. As with agriculture, this may pay dividends later.

In many cases the role of NGOs will be to deal with disease caused by contact with the wider world.

i. Contacts with members of national society that expose people to epidemics against which they have no immunity.

ii. Pressure on resources that affect nutrition.

iii. Changes in the environment that upset natural balances, as when water development introduces malaria.

iv. New sedentary lifestyles that facilitate the spread of communicable diseases and undermine subsistence activities.

People who are aware, or become aware, that their health standards have fallen for any of these reasons will be more willing to adopt new preventive measures.

3. Objectives of the community diagnosis

i. To involve the community in an analysis of the changes its members are undergoing and in a discussion of alternatives.

ii. To help the community to define its most urgent health needs within a changing situation.

iii. To inform non-indigenous personnel on general health conditions, attitudes to health, existing systems of treatment and people's expectations of any new health service.

iv. To inform the communities about the scope of NGO interventions, their need for a high level of participation, their constraints in terms of costs and their function within the health system of the state.

If the community diagnosis is approached with these broad objectives in mind rather than with narrow clinical or statistical considerations, participation is assured. The diagnosis should result in the formation of committees at community and inter-community level, even if these structures are initially simple in nature.

4. Priorities

i. Epidemics. It is essential to provide indigenous peoples with protection against the more virulent communicable diseases such as measles, whooping cough and diptheria. These can spread wildly within communities and over entire regions. Viral infections, such as the common cold and influenza, can also cause serious epidemics when isolated peoples are brought into contact; they rapidly bring on respiratory complaints and debilitate populations to such an extent that the people are no longer able to carry out subsistence activities. Vaccination campaigns are logistically complex. Cold-chains are particularly hard to maintain in remote areas. Refrigerators should be located in strategic communities and a member of the community made responsible for their operation. Communities should be forewarned of the arrival of the vaccinating team so that people from the surrounding area can assemble. Records should be kept carefully. An unexpected problem can arise when individuals in an indigenous group are not named, but rely on kinship terminology for identification. In these cases tags may be appropriate.

A priority in the training of village health workers must be the administration of appropriate drugs to combat epidemics of respiratory infections. The scale of epidemics of this type makes necessary the design of a standard treatment — such as injection with depot penicillin — that health workers can apply to large numbers of people in emergencies. Groups that receive adequate treatment need not suffer the drastic population loss often associated with contact, and can,within two or three years, acquire a certain immunity to the worst effects of common viruses.

Preventive measures against epidemics should be carried out at the same time, with particular attention to sanitation, nutrition and shelter.

ii. First aid. Curative services for infections, fractures, burns, cuts, conjunctivitis, scabies etc. are likely to be very much in demand and may fill the time of the village health worker. Training should be adequate to the task and sufficient stocks of medicine should be maintained at village level.

iii. Intestinal complaints. The accurate diagnosis and appropriate treatment of diarrhoea will have an immediate effect on mortality in indigenous communities, particularly for children. Priorities will be instruction in the use of rehydration therapy and the control of parasitosis, possibly by periodic treatment of the school population.

Sanitation is very important, but a community programme to dig latrines will be ineffective unless they are always used. As soon as possible, all human excreta must be discharged into a chosen safe location, such as a latrine; education and community commitment will be needed as well as construction.

iv. Control of endemic diseases. Indigenous peoples are likely to have a certain degree of resistance to diseases, such as malaria and yellow fever, that are endemic to their areas. This does not mean they do not suffer their effects, which may include high infant mortality.

v. Nutrition. Health projects will not achieve long-term improvements in indigenous communities unless they examine the problems that are causing sickness. Foremost among these is nutrition, which is often under severe pressure from external change. Prevention of malnutrition must be put first.

vi. Water. An adequate supply of safe water will, in conjunction with basic hygiene, contribute to everyone's basic health and comfort and will reduce or avoid many diseases. Most diseases suffered by indigenous peoples are related to water, sanitation and/or nutrition. An appropriate manual should be consulted on water and sanitation (see Background Reading, p.119) as mistakes can make the new state worse than the old.

vii. Mother/child. The highest risks in indigenous societies are always to the mother and child. While traditional childbirth techniques should not be discouraged, great loss of life can be avoided by anti-tetanus innoculation and by health education in the use of sterile implements for cutting the umbilical cord. The study of beliefs is very important here, as in many societies childbirth can be seen as highly polluting.

viii. Mental health. This can often present difficulties, since serious cases will require specialist help which may be unavailable. Fieldworkers must proceed with the utmost caution and sensitivity to local interpretations of "abnormal" mental states. Some peoples fear and reject the mentally ill, but more commonly there are traditional methods which may be superior to anything else available. In this sphere it may be best to leave well alone until a substantial familiarity with the society has been attained.

5. Infrastructure

Health attention to indigenous peoples that relies on occasional visits to an area and maintains no infrastructure in the villages will never deal adequately with health conditions. Visits will tend to be too short and may not coincide with periods of stress; training will also suffer and the emphasis is more likely to be on a curative than on a preventive approach; control of the service will ultimately lie outside the communities served. For all these reasons health services need to establish an infrastructure in the area capable of dealing with all but the most serious cases.

i. Health centre. All services will require a base at a strategic point in the indigenous area. There must be easy access both to the communities served and to the nearest administration centre. If the service is directed specifically towards the indigenous people, rather than a mixed population of settlers and indigenous people, then the base must be located on land indisputably owned by the indigenous people. The base should provide facilities for a clinic, storage space for medical supplies, training facilities, and workshops for whatever means of transport the service relies on. People will identify more closely with their health centre if they have taken part in its construction.

ii. Health posts. Each village needs a local construction to serve exclusively as the health post. It should be sufficiently spacious to shelter a refrigerator, a basic pharmacy, a set of scales and the records. Typically a two-room structure offers sufficient space for examinations and a waiting area. Health posts should be built with community labour.

iii. Transport. A mobile approach to health care, with constant supervision of health workers and frequent training sessions, demands an efficient transport system.

6. The difficulties of Primary Health Care services

Sickness is the greatest constraint faced by indigenous peoples adjusting to different patterns of life. It can overwhelm them on contact with outside society, and may later become a permanent burden as they gradually lose access to resources and are forced to shoulder the conditions borne by the rural poor in general. If NGOs are to confront the real reasons causing ill health they face a daunting task. They must therefore be content to aim for limited goals: they must allow the people to gain in confidence, and must always ensure that the goals respond to the people's needs. All sorts of difficulties will arise, of which only a few are presented here:

i. dependence on modern drugs and forms of treatment can rapidly develop, often far exceeding the capacity of the people to pay. Community pharmacies are often heavily in arrears of payment, although quacks may extract high prices for useless pharmaceuticals such as vitamin injections.

ii. the morale of health workers is frequently low, particularly where their work receives scant recognition from the community, or where the state refuses to recognise their skills and pay a salary. Conversely, when they are salaried they can become a new elite in their communities.

iii. programmes in indigenous communities frequently depend on the presence of volunteer doctors.

iv. for their success, Primary Health Care programmes require the participation of a highly motivated population. Unless they are accompanied by effective methods of mobilising the people, there is a tendency for participation to slacken as soon as health has improved, even marginally.

IX. Education

1. Literacy

Literacy teaching can be a highly enabling intervention, although it can also of course pave the way for external domination.

In India, the Girijan People's Association of Andhra Pradesh was formed by tribal leaders who themselves had been illiterate five years before. (Literacy had been brought to them by another NGO.) Now they have created village associations to solve common agricultural problems; they invest the surplus gained from joint marketing in bee keeping and experiments with new crops; they run day schools and night schools; they build check-dams. They responded to severe floods on the Godavari River by organising rescues, distributing food and rehousing the homeless. They are still very poor, and serve as a labour force for non-tribal peoples, but they begin to have some control over their lives.

2. Formal education

Formal education systems will not replace the indigenous need for training in skills; in combination, however, appropriate formal (school based) and non-formal (practical) education offer excellent opportunities to indigenous people. The potential of formal education can only be realised when the goal is not simply to impose national education policies but rather to strengthen the identification of the indigenous people to its group, its institutions and its environment. NGO financial and technical aid can make the difference between the willing acceptance of appropriate schooling and submission to the imposition of alien educational systems. As always, this may not be the perception of the indigenous people, who may see formal education as the route into national society: the larger Shipibo communities of the Ucayali River, Peru, reject bilingual education and insist that their children receive Spanish education from non-native teachers.

Where bilingual education is acceptable, NGOs can give support in several ways:

i. assisting groups to contact the Ministry of Education and apply for the establishment of schools.

ii. motivating indigenous students towards teaching as a career.

iii. paying bilingual teachers until the state covers salaries.

iv. supporting bilingual educational resource centres that prepare school materials and design locally appropriate curricula.

v. providing funds for scholarship schemes where indigenous peoples lack access to secondary or higher education.

Some indigenous groups may find their only access to appropriate education is via shortwave radio transmission. The isolated communities of the Ecuadorian Shuar peoples have successfully combined broadcasting with a system of bilingual teachers. Since 1972 the headquarters of the Shuar Federation in the frontier town of Sucua has beamed daily school programmes on shortwave to hundreds of settlements in the Ecuadorian jungle. Until then Shuar children had to travel up to five days on foot to Spanish-speaking boarding schools, where they lost contact with their families and culture for years at a time. Now nearly 4,000 elementary school students and 1,000 secondary pupils receive lessons in maths, reading, writing and history in their own language, without leaving home. Every settlement has a schoolhouse, built by the parents, in which the pupils and a Shuar teacher meet for five and a half hours a day. The teacher makes sure the children understand the lessons as they come over the air, and attends regular training sessions during the holidays at the Sucua centre. The programmes are designed by a team of 10 Shuar with advanced qualifications in education. Broadcasting in pairs, they ensure that Shuar children receive an education firmly grounded in their own culture, but which also prepares the most able to take up positions in the sophisticated Shuar Federation. As a result of this imaginative bilingual and bicultural project, isolated Shuar communities do not suffer educationally for their remoteness, unlike many other groups of the jungle. Nor do adult Shuar miss out. Afternoon programmes have reduced adult illiteracy to about 10 per cent, and the 12 hours of daily air time is filled out in early morning and evenings with Shuar cultural programmes.

X. Project infrastructure

1. The need for a base

Fieldworkers may start their projects with a period of intense mobility, travelling around the indigenous area, encouraging the people to discuss a future that involves some form of organisation to confront conditions of oppression. The itinerant fieldworker sleeps in villages, inspiring meetings and assemblies in longhouses,in schoolhouses or in the open air. But this first stage of project management must give way to more formal living arrangements for the fieldworker and an office for the new organisation. It is often at this stage of the need for infrastructure that non-religious NGOs confront just those difficulties that they most criticise in the approaches of, for example, missions. Missions that develop large-scale settlement sites deep in indigenous areas, with accommodation for the missionaries, air strips, aircraft hangars, radio links, well-equipped health posts, and schools, can hardly fail to dwarf the communities they serve in terms of wealth, structural solidity and technology. NGOs with a small-scale approach in indigenous terms are unlikely to accept the need for such extravagance or permanence, believing instead that the infrastructure should be no more complex or sophisticated than can be managed by the people themselves.

2. Size limits

The NGO fieldworker makes do with local forms of housing and transport. This ensures that the people regard him or her as a collaborator rather than a person come to solve their problems. It also shows the people that the means of overcoming their isolation is not beyond their own capabilities.

Project infrastructure must be carefully gauged to the service that is provided and should grow as the service proves itself viable and popular. It is almost always wrong to start a project by building an ambitious structure in the hope that a correspondingly fine service will automatically follow. The indigenous communities of the Amazon are full of handsome health posts, built with NGO and indeed state funds, that are closed or employed for other purposes such as housing.

3. Health posts

These can be made with local materials by the people, but the service will also require a base combined with a clinic. If the service is ultimately to be managed by the representative organisation of the group, then the base and clinic should be built close to the administrative centre of the organisation. It is however often difficult to know at the start of a project where the administrative centre will be five or ten years hence.

4. Administrative offices

Location of administration presents problems. Groups will need, for instance, to make contacts with officials, administer projects, co-ordinate with NGOs, and attend to the people's legal problems. The administrative centres of new indigenous organisations serve to establish a presence and reflect the group's new corporate existence, so style and scale of the structures are often crucial considerations for the indigenous people. The Ecuadorian Shuar Federation has a base in a non-indigenous town. This extensive complex benefits from road links to the capital city of Quito and houses such vital project infrastructure as the studios and transmitters of the bilingual education programme. Such successes are however offset by many failures. More often the services offered by the organisation do not justify the infrastructure.

5. Recommendations

It is always important to keep a sense of proportion in the size of these offices, as indigenous leaders can over-estimate their needs in the same way as planners in national society. When indigenous organisations set up offices in towns, fieldworkers also move; but it is important that they should not be too closely identified with the indigenous administration centre; they should seek independent housing.

XI. Indigenous organisations

1. Introduction

This manual has laid repeated stress on organisation. New institutions are necessary because the traditionally loose political organisation of indigenous people cannot confront the pressures to which many groups are now exposed; loyalties based on kinship make for strong local ties but do not naturally promote the kind of regional organisation necessary for defence. Only relatively sophisticated forms of organisation can enable indigenous peoples to make their voice heard, claim services due to them and gain control over the way they are carried out.

Even though the need for new institutions is often urgent, organisation building should be avoided as an end in itself. It must respond to the aspirations of the people and build on existing social structures.

2. Local organisations

These may be formed, for instance, when several extended families take advantage of existing legislation to claim legal recognition of a demarcated territory. In such circumstances the advantages of adopting a community organisation are clear. Institutions at this level may elect officials to negotiate with state agencies, maintain order, and manage communal enterprises and collective labour. Village level organisations are rarely as united or homogeneous as they appear at first sight.

i. dominant kinship groups often exploit services to their own ends.

ii. leaders may act as power brokers, controlling political influence and trade.

iii. priority groups such as women, widows and orphans are often voiceless.

These difficulties are met by ensuring that all initiatives at community level promote broad participation. Programme staff such as village health workers, extensionists and community store managers should not be chosen exclusively from the dominant groups and must be held accountable to the assembly.

No project should bypass the traditional older leaders just because they cannot, for instance, read and write in the national language. One method of power-sharing may be to build on the institutions that already exist for consultation, such as community meetings and assemblies. The effectiveness of these groups can be greatly increased by the formation of committees where the younger leaders, for instance, assume responsibility for carrying out decisions taken in assembly.

In the case of the Aguaruna and Huambisa Council, considered by many to be one of the most effective indigenous federations in South America, there have been problems with the bureaucratisation of power along generation lines. The Council has managed to avoid many of the pitfalls through long and fruitful public debate, institutionalised through repeated assemblies.

Projects intended to include traditional authority in the sharing of new power will have to be guided to include not only older men but also women, both old and young, throughout the whole process. There is obviously a certain conflict between respecting traditional power (which often favours men) and not exacerbating gender differences when trying to introduce new tools and knowledge, and thus new power, to an indigenous society.

3. Regional organisations

These are usually combinations of communities that unite to devise defensive strategies. These organisations can be particularly effective in applying pressure locally in defence of the communities' joint interests and, in the best cases, in administering their own change. Their success depends largely on the strength of village-level organisations and on the coordination between their representatives. Areas of support for regional organisations include:

i. the promotion of solidarity. Action may involve, for instance, a general land titling programme that requires coordination between communities.

ii. overcoming problems of communication between widely dispersed communities.

iii. encouraging contacts between regional organisations and representatives of state agencies for the provision of appropriate services.
iv. legal recognition of regional organisations is often problematic, and can be helped by legal assistance and training.
v. long-term funding may take time to achieve. The Aguaruna and Huambisa Council in Peru uses the profits of centralised marketing and other income-generating projects, including a snake farm (for serum) which was initially NGO-supported.

4. National organisations

These bring together indigenous peoples with differing cultural characteristics. Inter-ethnic representation of this type seeks to influence policy at a national level by developing common platforms on such crucial issues as land rights, services, recognition of indigenous languages and organisations etc. In the last 15 years new indigenous institutions have developed to such an extent in Colombia, Ecuador, Peru, Bolivia and Brazil that it would be unthinkable to discuss indigenous affairs without reference to their federations. NGO support for them takes various forms:
i. capital sums to help acquire office space and accommodation for leaders visiting the capital city. Such buildings should be multi-purpose, acting additionally as housing and cultural centres for scholarship students, providing space for meetings and training courses, etc.
ii. counterpart core funding for salaries of rotating teams of leaders.
iii. scholarship schemes for the higher education of students proposed by the member organisations.
iv. inter-ethnic training courses for indigenous managers of services.
v. legal assistance and land titling programmes.

NGOs supporting organisations need to ensure that the activities respond to the grass-roots needs of the indigenous people and that preoccupations at national level do not distance the leaders from their communities. They should discourage long periods of residence by leaders in the capital (which might lead to their "citification"), and promote frequent field visits. They should also be aware that cultural differences between groups can make for friction in national organisations; they should try to ensure that no single group dominates.

5. International organisations

The common interests and shared problems of national federations have helped to overcome the previous isolation of many indigenous groups, enabling them to form associations that transcend national boundaries. One is the Coordinating Group of the Amazon, which brings together national federations from Peru, Ecuador, Colombia, Brazil and Bolivia to discuss common policy at regular intervals. The value to the indigenous peoples of a self-managed organisation at international level lies in the direct access to national governments and international institutions that indigenous leaders can claim when high-level policy decisions affect their people unfavourably. However, indigenous organisations that function at international level run the risk of losing touch with their peoples, and there is clearly a danger of new forms of representation recreating old structures of dependence unless these growing organisations can maintain participation.

6. Pitfalls

The fieldworker's motivating role has in many cases been crucial in introducing the organisational approach. However the approach has not always been successful, particularly where elaborate organisations are apparently run by indigenous peoples but actually depend entirely on fieldworkers and the financial backing behind them. Some of the obvious pitfalls are:

i. over-sophisticated organisational models. To be beneficial, organisation must be appropriate to the particular needs of the people. Complex national and international organisations should not neglect the need to first establish a basic organisation in groups that may, for instance, be mobile, and monolingual and may have no formed communities.

ii. a paternalistic attitude to organisation-building. If the fieldworker assumes people will benefit by adopting an organisational form designed by him/herself, the resulting operation will not be viable. Fieldworkers must collaborate in, rather than direct, the search for culturally acceptable forms of representation. Their prime role will be as trainers in the necessary management skills.

iii. faulty social analysis. Fieldworkers who unquestioningly promote organisations or social structures that appear to be egalitarian may reinforce injustices and effectively exclude people from participation and power-sharing.

iv. seeking to control the organisational process. Intermediary organisations frequently have a vested interest in preserving an advisory role with indigenous organisations. This can lead their fieldworkers to resist attempts by the indigenous leadership to manage its own affairs. On these occasions NGOs can fund the representative organisations directly, thus avoiding dependence on intermediaries for the expenses of arranging meetings, mounting courses, bringing services to member communities, etc. NGOs need to recognise the point at which intermediaries have outlived their usefulness and should resist local professional opinion that insists on making funding conditional on the retention of advisers.

Julio Etchart

Amazon Peoples' delegation in London
'The value to the indigenous peoples of a self-managed organisation at international level lies in the direct access to national governments and international institutions...' (page 96).

XII. Solidarity

The development of indigenous peoples' own organisations over the last generation has been complemented by the growth of non-governmental support groups. This began in the 1960s, with the formation of the International Work Group for Indigenous Peoples, in Denmark, and of Survival International, in Britain. A handful of similar organisations was formed in western Europe and North America during the 1970s, though many have since been dissolved. (For a full list see Goodland, 1982; details at the end of this manual.)

Most of those which remain work in broadly similar ways: they appeal directly to governments, companies and others who are violating the rights of indigenous peoples; they raise the issues at, for instance, the United Nations; they produce publications; they support field projects; they press for better laws; and they run educational programmes about indigenous peoples, their value, and the threats which they face. The differences between organisations are determined by size, source of funds and leading objective. Many of the larger organisations are funded at least in part by governments, which can bring the degree of their independence into question. The arena is complex, and conflict is a possibility.

Some support organisations have a more academic approach while others appeal to a more popular audience. The largest of the latter is Survival International, which has an "urgent action" network similar to that formed by Amnesty International in support of prisoners of conscience. (Survival has supporters in some 50 countries and offices in the UK, France, Spain and the USA.) Survival International and other organisations have had some success in changing attitudes in governments, companies and international banks, and even some success in changing projects.

FIELD METHODS

I. Introduction

The role of the fieldworker varies according to the needs of the group in question, and particularly to the extent to which it has developed institutions for dealing with national society. It is not the sophistication of traditional organisation that is important, but the external relations. Some groups have achieved broad socio-political representation and participation and can mobilise to relate to national society; some are experimenting in this direction; some have no means of engaging as a group with the wider world. These distinctions will make all the difference to the fieldworker's task.

II. Limitations of non-governmental organisations

Where the indigenous group does not have an organisation through which it can relate to national society, many tasks devolve on the NGO. Those groups which are weaker in external relations are both more in need of NGO assistance and more at risk of being harmed by the NGO.

1. Being "charitable"

The "charitable" nature of some NGOs, e.g. some church groups, can be a pitfall leading to paternalism and dependence, since it may distort direct work with indigenous people. The motivation and perhaps the funding of the NGO must not lead to "charitable" relations with indigenous groups. It may seem heartless to deny requests from people who make known their needs; it may be tempting to gain the control in human relations that charity affords; the group may skilfully manoeuvre the NGO into playing patron in the traditional, destructive manner, since that is familiar and understood. Withholding of gifts may be seen as selfish and even disrespectful, as a denial of equality to the indigenous people, but gifts must be between equals. In the long run, it is essential that the relationship be enabling, not a demoralising restatement of patronage created by misguided generosity. Again, the risk of patronage is much greater with groups with less organisation for external affairs.

2. Being radical

Some groups, especially the less formalised ones, may be urgently in need of rescue, but radical action on their behalf can be as destructive as charitable patronage. Indigenous peoples may not be willing to reveal to NGOs the degree of their long-term interest in maintaining good relations with their patrons. Patrons or local bosses may have much greater strength than short-term NGO representatives, missionaries or even indigenous federations. They may control local power, credit, access to inputs and advice, transport, access to market, health care and possibly justice; they may be sources of protection as well as violence. Indigenous people will not be willing to dispense with this power structure, or to confront it, unless there is a long-term alternative that can serve them as well. Even where indigenous people encourage fieldworkers to take a radical line, this situation must be carefully assessed. They may "betray" the fieldworkers in the interests of their own survival.

Fieldworkers seeking to undermine the influence of the local power structure over indigenous peoples must be certain that the institutional support from NGOs will be there for as long as it is needed. The fieldworker must have the appropriate skills (a good legal understanding will be essential) and be confident that he or she is not encouraging people to take unwise risks. The people must be fully aware of the implications of action. Fieldworkers may need to help channel a combative spirit into legally acceptable forms of defence, especially with groups which have not developed organisations for confronting national society. Where organisations exist, they will already have created some alternative to the local power structure and will be continually challenging it; the NGO role is more likely to be help with engaging lawyers, and the group itself will focus on issues and plan strategy. The NGO has less opportunity to cause disaster than with groups lacking organisation. Even more sensitive judgment is called for when national society draws indigenous peoples into criminal action.

The local power structure may exist on the margins of the law, as in the case of the smugglers of cocaine who have widely infiltrated the hills and valleys of the Amazon basin's high jungle region. Indigenous peoples in these areas run grave risks of becoming caught as victims in the web of the complex relations between authorities and traffickers. Indigenous people will certainly witness the traffickers' operations and may also be aware of police movements; this knowledge makes them dangerous to both sides. At lower altitudes, they have grown coca for millenia and may be bribed to extend

their plantings; in Colombia, one penalty for being caught is confiscation of land. Chewing coca is traditional and widespread, so that the basic commodity is familiar, although it requires considerable processing to change it into the marketable drug; coca chewers do not ingest cocaine. Commercial production of the leaf is illegal but profitable; large monetary rewards are offered for help with smuggling, such as the use of a village airstrip or the harbouring of a processing laboratory. Processing may attract punitive and murderous military raids. NGO fieldworkers must leave security decisions in the hands of the indigenous authorities and limit their role to encouraging awareness of the dangers of involvement with the cocaine trade, and promoting discussion of alternative income generating activities, although unfortunately nothing is likely to be commercially comparable at present.

III. Know the people

1. Basic information
Since indigenous peoples are so radically different in cultural terms from dominant societies it is particularly important to have a close knowledge of their traditions and cultural beliefs. Knowing about indigenous people involves first and foremost questioning one's own assumptions and adopting a frame of mind that admits the validity of the unfamiliar. Otherwise the fieldworker will merely apply to the situation the prejudices and personal training of his or her own culture. Outsiders need imagination to envisage the real and ramifying effects of their actions; they need to think about the causal chain which follows from them. Specifically the fieldworker needs to learn about the following features.

i. The language. The groups with least organisation for dealing with national society may also be those whose culture is most unfamiliar. They may be largely monolingual, so that fieldworkers require a knowledge of the indigenous language. This should be learnt as early as possible, so as to reduce dependence on interpreters and assure broad contact with the people. Learning the people's language will be much less of a priority when more of the population is likely to be bilingual, and needs will already have been defined.

ii. The context. There are many details that should always be sought, so far as they are known, before departure for the field, to avoid long periods spent repeating the discovery of information already known. State offices, university libraries, geographical societies and missionary archives will all provide relevant material if this has not already been edited and made accessible by intermediary organisations. Essential information includes:

a. cadastral surveys of lands.

b. estimations of land use capability.

c. development plans for the region as a whole.

d. educational infrastructure.

e. health conditions as known by the relevant health authority.

iii. The degree of integration into national society. This will be revealed in part by the recorded material mentioned above, but more immediately by direct knowledge of the group. Fieldworkers with no previous experience of indigenous peoples will have difficulties in correctly estimating the degree of integration of a particular group, and will need to visit various groups as early as possible in order to gain a comparative perspective. The advice of anthropologists should also be sought.

iv. The division of labour by gender and age. Fieldworkers will be particularly interested in knowing how the division of labour has been changed by the group's relations with national society. This will give an indication of the likely impact of any further innovations that may be implemented by the NGO, and particularly of their effect on women.

v. Religion and its effect on priorities. For religion and for concepts of causality, anthropological studies are an important source. The whole understanding of life may be alien to the fieldworker in ways initially difficult to recognise.

vi. The management of authority. Fieldworkers will need to investigate closely the existing leadership structures, including decision-making processes, institutions, degree of representation, the exercise of power and means of resolving disputes.

vii. Non-indigenous relations. The fieldworker must discover as soon as possible just how the group regards its association with missionaries, local authorities, patrons, commercial concerns and competitors for its resources. These relations will often be more complex than appears at first sight. The indigenous people may well express distaste for non-indigenous peoples in general and encourage the fieldworker to feel that he or she alone is acceptable to them. Uncritical acceptance of this may lead the fieldworker into hostility to non-indigenous people that may interfere with his or her capacity to work effectively. It is always wise to reserve comment on other non-indigenous people in the general area even while attempting to make the people aware of any injustices to which they may be exposed.

It is particularly important to distinguish between local and national structures of oppression, since different reactions are required. Work in support of indigenous peoples can become impossible where oppression at local level is supported by the state. Where favourable legislation exists fieldworkers should encourage good relations between indigenous peoples and the state through their representative organisations, as a means of defending their interests against local forms of domination.

viii. Action-research. Fieldworkers cannot be expected to learn all this instantly. They are frequently pressed for time and there may be an urgent need for a specific project. Action-research is a successful method used to inform the fieldworker on, for instance, power relations in an indigenous community. The "action" refers to small-scale projects which allow the people to participate in new ways while "research" is the analysis of the exercise made by the fieldworker while gradually learning which topics are important for the group. In this method both action and research elements must be flexible, so as to adjust to new information as it becomes apparent. Fieldworkers are warned against expecting ever to "understand" a people fully. They must adopt an essentially open-ended and open-minded attitude to their research.

ix. Culture. This manual has emphasised how closely integrated are the facets of indigenous lives. The fieldworker has first to learn how to behave and how to identify rapidly the rules which must not be transgressed. Beyond that, it will take years to acquire a grasp of social mores or the likely effect of religion in decisions over production. There may be customs that the fieldworker may find deeply repugnant, or perhaps just difficult to relate to. Not all such difficulties can be overcome with time. Examples might be peoples for whom extended drunkenness has religious and social importance, or hallucinogenic drugs, or the mutilation of girls. The fieldworker cannot expect always to find other cultures attractive. The effects of change compound this, as any people undergoing acute stress may also be suffering a breakdown of traditional restraints on anti-social behaviour. Listening, learning, and understanding will all be rewarding in themselves and will pay dividends in future work, but to assume that they will solve all problems is romantic and unhelpful. Culture shock is often a very real problem for fieldworkers and should be treated as realistically as possible.

2. Ask the people

Clearly those best able to provide information are the people themselves. Gathering information from indigenous people needs tact and patience. Personal relations are of the greatest importance to many indigenous people and conversations that sustain them are a key means of socialising; fieldworkers pressing for "hard" information may infringe etiquette among people who restrict such conversations to immediate kin. Relations of trust

Amuesha People, Peru
'Personal relations are of the greatest importance to many indigenous people and conversations that sustain them are a key means of socialising.' (page 103).

Luke Holland, Survival International

are essential for any direct questioning and the formality of standard survey techniques, for instance, is quite inappropriate.

i. Choose questions with care. Indigenous people are often reluctant to enter into details of their lives with strangers . Indeed, it is a measure of the insensitivity of most national societies that this should come as a surprise to the incoming fieldworker. Some indigenous societies with powerful negotiating organisations have chosen to reject research anthropologists, as in the "research workers crisis" of the Trobriand Islands, Papua New Guinea. People will tend to regard inquisitiveness with suspicion, particularly from fieldworkers whose area of enquiry does not obviously coincide with their reason for being with the group. Traditional peoples may respond to questioning by evasiveness or may simply say in reply what the questioner seems to want. The fieldworker therefore must:

a. find a balance between a curiosity that appeals to the group and one that arouses suspicion.

b. reflect on people's comments on specific situations and try to gauge their reactions without constantly asking questions.

c. develop techniques for initiating open-ended discussions.

ii. Respect people's beliefs. In different places people have different beliefs about life. Fieldworkers may find some of these beliefs so unfamiliar as to think of them as "wrong" or "fantastical". Whether, for example, what we refer to as "witchcraft" really exists is not the point. The point is that, in a place where the majority of people believe in its existence, it will operate and the fieldworker would do well to respect it. Looking at it in this way, people's motivations can be more clearly understood and collaboration with them can be that much more effective. However, fieldworkers should also be warned against going too far in their adoption of local beliefs; in other social contexts, for instance if the fieldworker visits the capital city, it can be most unsettling when new beliefs do not operate in a place that ought to be familiar. The disturbing nature of this experience should not be underestimated.

iii. Avoid criticism. Where general information is not available in the form of newspapers and other publications, rumours can be very powerful. Great care must be taken in voicing opinions since these will spread wide, and probably in a garbled form, along the local grapevine. Public criticism of any indigenous person by a fieldworker can for this reason cause bitter feelings of resentment. Indigenous people may criticise each other behind their backs but they will strongly resent the criticism if it comes from an outsider.The sensitivity to criticism may become particularly acute among indigenous groups that are experimenting with new forms of organisation. In these situations it should be the task of the fieldworker to help establish mechanisms by which rivalries threatening to break out from under the surface can be channelled into institutional energies. Many projects founder on violent personal recriminations that could have been avoided by a more sensitive approach.

iv. Feed information back. The objective of information gathering must be to make the people aware of their own situation. This can only be achieved by involving the people directly in the process, encouraging them to voice their own opinions about their problems. By feeding back to the people the results of the fieldworker's own investigations, the group is in a position to design a plan of action related both to its situation and to the external context. This insures against partial solutions that ignore either the wishes of the people or the situation of the group within national society.

3. Gender of fieldworker

The education and the work of women fieldworkers earn them the respect that indigenous men generally reserve for other males. They therefore may have access to the worlds of both women and men, and this gives them a unique opportunity to gain the confidence of women whose needs and feelings are generally ignored in "development planning." Working with women will always tend to be difficult, even for a woman, because indigenous women are less likely to be bilingual than their menfolk and may be less used to expressing their needs and seeking remedies. Women fieldworkers should accept the challenge and never limit their interventions to the men, since this would merely confirm the low opinions of themselves that the women are too apt to accept from national society.

Non-indigenous men will not have the same facility for crossing the genders at will. Indigenous men will expect them to work exclusively with men. Since all planned change must meet equally the problems of both sexes it is always advisable for fieldworkers to operate in teams of men and women. Health and agricultural training, for instance, when carried out by male staff, will inevitably exclude the female population. Where women are the subsistence farmers, there is little sense in continuing the practice of sending only male fieldworkers to work with them. The same applies to health and nutrition. Even in industrialised societies, women are the caretakers of basic health; preventive medicine and much care will always depend on women, even where, as in Nepal, both "modern" and "traditional" medicine are exclusively in male hands.

Women should be warned that their independence will tend to suffer in the eyes of indigenous peoples when they are part of a team, even as wife or partner to a male fieldworker. The people will assume that all decisions are made by the man and will therefore choose to deal more closely with him. The woman fieldworker should at an early stage make clear her own areas of responsibility and insist on direct lines of communication with the indigenous people.

4. Understand indigenous leadership
On starting work, fieldworkers must give priority to investigating the nature of indigenous leadership structures. They must always remember that organisations created by indigenous people are not political parties or economic cooperatives, but associations of people, often grounded in kinship. This means that politics, organisation and leadership are highly personal. Many interventions have failed through lack of understanding of the arrangements for power sharing; these frequently are often the opposite of the type of democratic motivation the fieldworker would like to see in operation. Even when the eventual objective is to encourage forms of democratic expression within the group, the fieldworker needs to respect the existing system through an understanding of its workings and history.

i. Groups without some form of representative organisation will pose a special problem. Authority will be scattered as widely as the extended family groups, lineages or other traditional forms of social organisation. People will relate to NGOs and their representatives as they do to each other: along the lines of family or clan interests. Fieldworkers will be valued by competing factions as a source of outside power, and they should be warned that it is virtually impossible to avoid taking sides. The NGO will spend much time simply trying to distribute the attention of its representatives evenly on all sides. The only strategy available is to be aware of the effects of their presence on the people, and take it into account in any further planning.

ii. Fieldworkers with groups beginning to relate more formally to national society will need to look at immediate history. Government policy may have established indigenous leaders for its administrative convenience. Missionaries may have co-opted the children of key figures in a given society for education according to their own criteria. Previous programmes may have created employment opportunities that have given prestige to leadership. Salaried indigenous teachers, for instance, often create a new elite. If such processes have been in force for more than a generation the relations of leadership and subordination within the group are likely to be highly complex. The fieldworker arriving in such a situation is likely to be co-opted by a given leader and his supporters, especially a marginal leader who has most to gain from outside support. This will greatly complicate future efforts to bring in democratic power sharing. It is particularly difficult to assess at first how representative the existing organisation is. Great care must be taken not to reinforce the domination of the people by a group such as male elders whose power may no longer be checked by traditional structures.

iii. Groups with more formal organisations will probably have overcome the problem of representativeness and power sharing to a much greater extent. But, even where power is shared more broadly and decision-making is vested, for instance, in village assemblies, there may be a tendency for leadership to remain in the hands of a reduced number of privileged families. Impartiality is essential, particularly where leaders are elected periodically, since interference will be deeply resented. Fieldworkers may concentrate instead on supporting disadvantaged sectors within the society, such as women and children.

iv. Recommendations.

a. Fieldworkers should avoid forming close personal relationships with any particular local leader. This will tend to isolate them from competing factions.

b. They should not attempt to democratise non-representative institutions by establishing new ones, favouring opposition leaders. It is always preferable to seek broader participation within an existing institution.

c. They must exercise extreme caution in nominating all types of leaders, such as village health workers, teachers or agricultural extensionists. Outside support to an individual may be sufficient to establish a new life-long leader — not necessarily the right one.

d. They must take steps to counteract the tendency of existing leaders to nominate themselves or members of their kin groups to new positions of responsibility. It is better to work in projects with the entire community so that the indigenous people themselves can identify those most committed for positions of responsibility.

e. They should seek to ensure that decision-making on projects is firmly in the hands of local assemblies, in which all traditional authority figures are represented.

f. They can promote educational opportunities to make more potential leaders available in the future.

g. If the group has no overall leadership, the fieldworker will need to avoid vesting control in the hands of one segment. It may be necessary to ensure that each segment or kin group has independent control over its own resources.

IV. Golden rules

1. Be committed

Field work with indigenous people calls for a high degree of commitment. It is necessary to carry the fieldworker through the physical and emotional discomforts that are standard project fare. The type of fieldwork recommended in this manual is long-term, and will not afford more creature comforts as the years go by. Fieldworkers will be expected to share the conditions of life of the people; work will be hard, with only short breaks outside the area; frequent sickness can be expected, especially while adjusting to a new climate and diet; wages are likely to be at subsistence levels; increasing identification with indigenous people over long periods of fieldwork can distance people from their own cultures. These circumstances are only tolerable to people with a high level of commitment to the indigenous group involved, and with a long-term commitment to the cause of indigenous people in general.

Since the welfare of indigenous groups is so often threatened by powerful forces reflecting local, national and international realities it is likely that there will be many disappointments. Further disappointments that may place a strain on the fieldworker's commitment and lead to disillusionment will include, for instance, programmes that fail for technical or social reasons that could have been foreseen; or rejection of the intervention because of internal divisions within the group.

Commitment must be tempered with a philosophical attitude towards the real possibilities for long-term improvement in conditions. In spite of their multiple problems indigenous peoples very rarely give way to misery; they live for the present, enjoy themselves and give themselves time (in what can appear outright wastefulness) to reach decisions or achieve goals. Fieldworkers with a more sophisticated understanding of the pressures bearing down on the group should not allow their commitment to its welfare to override all other considerations. For although indigenous people will appreciate honest commitment and unselfish concern for their wellbeing, they will not respect a humourless or defeatist view of life.

2. Remember first impressions

Fieldworkers growing accustomed to the conditions under which they live with an indigenous group will also tend to grow to accept these conditions with the same sense of fatalism as the people themselves. It is therefore important to retain a fresh image of the first few weeks spent in actively getting to know the situation of the group and forming personal impressions from sight and hearsay. These impressions will be of great value in the future, as yardsticks by which to measure change and its effects on the people. The arrival of a fieldworker in an area may inspire the people to unusual levels of joint activity; this show of communal spirit and harmony will most likely subside shortly afterwards, but it is an indication of the potential of the group.

Fieldworkers must also take steps to avoid becoming "stale" or inflexible through isolation. They can, for instance, foster links with other fieldworkers, arrange for periodic meetings during rest periods in urban centres, and visit other projects. They should communicate regularly with researchers, university departments and pressure groups and seek to maintain an area of research of their own that is independent of the programme.

3. Go in gently
The fieldworker who hopes to discover the needs of the people and encourage them to identify these for themselves before going on to take their own action, will need to slow down on arrival in the group's territory, since their pace of life is bound to be much slower. Unless the new fieldworker adapts his or her rhythm, the group will lose the initiative. The fieldworker will begin to impose solutions rather than allow these to arise. NGOs that accept the need for periods of investigation before the start of a new project tacitly recognise the need for a slow entry into the indigenous world. The task, finally, is to work with the group, not to add to the knowledge of the outside world. Prior investigation should not be too protracted. It must always be borne in mind that the objective of the recommended action-research method is to make the fieldworker an effective catalyst for the growing self-management of the group's new situation. A balance needs to be found between taking a culturally acceptable, easy approach and not losing sight of the primary purpose. Fieldworkers should not be surprised when their sensitive approach is not shared by officials such as government extension agents. These may well commit all the cultural errors possible, such as making a brief and low profile appearance, imposing solutions, rejecting discussion, showing little respect for indigenous language and no patience for indigenous technology — yet, in spite of all these solecisms, they may still be received with respect and obeyed. Many indigenous people have a deep respect for government authority, and will accept dramatic changes in their lives through government directives. To officials and others who have been in the area a long time, a new fieldworker will appear naive and idealistic. The fieldworker should not ignore government officials with local experience just because of disagreement with their aims. They may be invaluable sources of information.

4. Avoid creating false hopes
It is very easy to underestimate the difficulty of overcoming the disadvantages faced by indigenous peoples. Given the strength of the local power structure, of discrimination and of economic subordination, fieldworkers may well be misled by initial enthusiasm and may be led to

promise improvements they cannot in fact implement. Indigenous people have been offered many different programmes over their years of contact with society, and experience has taught them that few of the promises materialise. They remember the promises and hold any failure to abide by them against the fieldworker whose future credibility with the group is then endangered. The fieldworker should always hold enthusiasm in check and, rather than make promises or mount grandiose projects, encourage the people to confront and overcome their difficulties through their own resources.

5. Start small and be patient

Just as it is important to enter an indigenous area with tact and learn how to recognise needs, it is equally vital to start programmes with some small-scale activities and not launch immediately into a large project. The fieldworker should not try to attack all the visible problems at once, but adopt a carefully-planned and relaxed approach to individual problem areas, allowing plenty of time for discussion, participation and feedback. Resist pressures to produce results if this will mean launching into frantic activity. It must be accepted that work with many groups is on such a long-term basis that individuals may well not see the results of their efforts. They should certainly not be tempted to force the pace to gratify their own aspirations for the group. The best method will be slow and patient training, constantly encouraging the people and their leaders to consider their situation and the possibilities for action.

Promote use of local resources. If the fieldworker's goal is to work with knowledge and resources already available then great patience will be required to elicit from the people exactly what assets they already possess; they may well claim to have none and expect instead to be provided with everything from outside. Fieldworkers will frequently have to face a growing lack of interest in indigenous technology as exposure to external influences demeans it in indigenous eyes. They should certainly not reinforce this by promoting non-indigenous technology too hard.

6. Encourage participation

i. Support traditional activities. Even where there are no formal "organisations" for external purposes, indigenous peoples will have their own forms of participation whether in joint fishing parties, work groups or social reunions with possible ritual significance. Fieldworkers can show their respect for these forms of organisation by taking part when invited: thus they will learn how best to encourage less traditional forms that they hope to introduce, such as:
a. regular meetings to discuss priorities.

b. communal income-generating activities to pay for services.

c. work parties to create or maintain village infrastructure.

Fieldworkers must be aware that these new activities may take time that would otherwise be spent on domestic production. They cannot expect people to give project participation higher priority than subsistence. New activities must therefore:

a. fit the particular subsistence economy.

b. not kill enthusiasm by overwork. Where the communal work party is a tradition, as it is in much of rural South America, fieldworkers must resist temptations to overuse its potential for projects. They should also bear in mind the social function of the work party and never force the pace of work.

c. use available time effectively. Fieldworkers can help with forward planning so that people engaging in unfamiliar activities know about the task in hand and do not become frustrated.

ii. Help to organise meetings. Until people hold regular meetings the fieldworker may well need to help plan and coordinate assemblies. Their role of catalyst is essential in:

a. making the concept and mechanism of meetings familiar to the people.

b. formulating options for discussion.

c. training in methods of debating, voting, recording decisions etc.

d. helping to design means of implementing decisions.

Fieldworkers encouraging new forms of participation must take great care not to dominate the proceedings. Many groups, for instance, will be quite unfamiliar with public debate and may be influenced by any strong speaker. Indigenous assemblies that have not been adequately prepared to function as decision-making institutions are especially vulnerable to persuasive government agents. Fieldworkers can help inexperienced groups to overcome this vulnerability by regular assemblies that discuss and plan small-scale projects with which the people are immediately familiar. Once decisions have been taken and implemented on a small scale over a period of time, assemblies of indigenous peoples will have the confidence to examine more controversial issues.

iii. Recognise bottlenecks. The process of channelling participation into effective forms of popular organisation is rarely straightforward with indigenous peoples. Fieldworkers frequently react to the problems by simply ignoring them and pressing on with the particular project in hand in the hope that questions of representation and participation will resolve themselves. They should recognise instead that these situations arise where the process described above has been wrongly implemented through either haste or over-enthusiasm. Where efforts at increasing participation have merely resulted, for instance, in rendering leadership structures more rigid, fieldworkers face a difficult choice. They can accept the status quo and maintain good relations with the existing leadership, or they can attempt to broaden the base of participation and run the risk of endangering the project.In these cases it is always advisable to return to first principles. By starting the process afresh and encouraging participation in small-scale projects that bring people together around a subject of common interest, the fieldworker can also inspire the organisation to renew a commitment to its constituencies. It is never advisable to solve problems of low participation by promoting splinter groups or alternative organisations since these can cause serious divisions and merely confuse the issues further in the minds of the people.

7. Train on the job

Training for indigenous groups has traditionally concentrated on imparting vocational or life skills to small groups of individuals within communities, assuming that isolated courses in, for example, carpentry, mechanics, latrine building or sewing, can equip the people to face changing circumstances. This manual has tried to show that the objectives of training must be much broader than this simple transfer of technology, and must supply those specific skills that the individual group needs in order to manage its own affairs. We have already looked at the methods of encouraging people towards solidarity, participation and self-reliance through dialogue, assemblies and, eventually, organisation and we have said that a vital part of this process is the identification of small-scale projects which can be the concrete expression of the group's new form of organisation. How is training for these projects to be implemented? (See also manuals recommended at the end of this book.)

i. Loosely structured groups. Reinforce existing knowledge. Great care must be taken to find out about indigenous technology, so that the new skills to be introduced can be made to complement rather than oppose existing knowledge. An agronomist, for instance, will avoid aggressively promoting his or her technology during training. It is most important that fieldworkers resist attempts to slot them into traditional "teacher" roles, and that they encourage the people to view training and learning as mutual investigation and a sharing of knowledge.

Seeing is believing. To help to demystify training much of the work should be done in an informal setting — in the cattle camp, in the fields, in the shade of a tree or in a traditional meeting place. The people will learn mainly by seeing and doing, so training should go hand in hand with practical implementation of the technology. The trainer should use the time spent in walking between gardens and homes, or resting, to encourage the people to reflect on what they have seen or done. Simple visual aids, such as the flannel-graph, will help keep attention.

Work with the whole community. Training can also be incorporated into everyday activities, as for instance in the communal work group, which can be associated with an innovative practice. Again, rest groups can provide an opportunity for discussion, but it is the regular community assembly that gives most scope for dialogue. People who have taken part in the work session will have a personal interest in the project, and that will give them the confidence to speak their minds. Leaders gain experience in organising communal work and respecting joint decisions.

Training for such groups therefore concentrates on helping the people mobilise their own resources and manpower in new ways. There is little attempt at introducing sophisticated technology that requires specialisation among the people, since this would deter general participation, but health care workers, for instance, may be trained. The method is slow and does require long-term, consistent and sensitive fieldwork. But it also promotes community solidarity and provides the essential base for further, more complex interventions.

ii. More formal groups. Communities that have developed basic structures for channelling participation can begin to develop more complex projects such as communal marketing facilities or health services; leaders require more intensive training, and project staff also need to be selected for a degree of skill specialisation. These activities should never develop at the expense of community participation, and training must involve methods of ensuring the accountability of programme staff. Fieldworkers may have their own ideas, for instance about potential project staff, but they should always respect the people's wishes when it comes to their election.

In-service training is the best. People learn new skills best when training is closely related to the duties they need to carry out. Thus marketing skills are gained by operation of, for instance, a village store. It is not always possible to arrange for the close supervision necessary for in-service training over a number of communities, so a degree of centralisation is often called for. This involves either establishing a pilot project in a strategic community where people can assemble for training, or organising courses. In both cases, community-level workers will need to come together frequently for training, and also to be visited by the trainers in their communities. Courses are not a sufficient training method for indigenous groups; they are effective only as a back-up to supervised in-service training.

Training courses need to be specifically designed for the group in question, and fieldworkers should develop innovative teaching skills such as role-playing, drama and use of models made from local materials.

114

iii. Groups with their own organisations take on a large part of the responsibility for planning training courses for their programme leaders. They choose the trainers and decide what is to be taught, when, where and to whom. Instructors should realise that their pupils will have considerable practical experience and will have attended a number of previous courses designed to upgrade their skills. Trainers should encourage a participatory approach, drawing on the experience of pupils to identify problem areas.

8. Keep self-reliance in view

Interventions in indigenous communities, whatever form they may take, should have a common theme — that is they should all lead towards self-management by instilling the skills and enthusiasm required for it. Keeping this theme in full view gives purpose and prevents an intervention from becoming purely charitable. Indeed, without this common theme the justification for intervention is much less clear. This means that fieldworkers need to evaluate the individual projects within a programme not just in terms of viability but also for their potential in increasing autonomy. Often the specific project fails but the group as a whole benefits from the experience of having organised around an issue. A basically sound programme can afford some failures as long as the main theme functions soundly.

9. Plan to withdraw

The commitment to phase out fieldworkers and, eventually, outside sources of funding is the main difference between NGO interventions that aim at self-management and those that encourage dependence. Methods of doing it will vary, but in general NGOs have to accept that withdrawing from involvement in indigenous groups is more difficult than with other social groups. The reasons for this include the slow pace of the work and the high degree of specialisation required of fieldworkers. It may well take a fieldworker one or two years to become familiar with the people, their environment, their problems and their particular needs. Projects themselves can be very long term. Bonds often develop between a group and the fieldworker. Though slow to trust outsiders, indigenous peoples may form strong attachments to fieldworkers they have come to know. The success of a given project can depend on the rapport established. These and other conditions mean that phasing out fieldworkers is likely to be a problem area. For this reason the question of withdrawal must be considered early and incorporated into the planning stage of the project.

Indigenous peoples with no representative organisation will be reluctant to condone the phasing out of fieldworkers who have been the main factors in altering their lives for what they see as the better. Before withdrawing, fieldworkers need to consider carefully whether the people are fully capable of administering the changes brought about, and provision needs to be made for follow up for many years after the intervention. Follow up will give support to, for example, bilingual teachers, village health-workers and indigenous leaders.

Groups that have structured communities, channels of marketing or limited health and education services, will also encourage fieldworkers to remain with them even though the group has resolved many of its problems of adjustment to national society. Fieldworkers will be especially highly regarded by the people in those types of society with an exploitative local leadership. Phase out in these situations can be sudden if leaders react to new demands made on them by expelling the fieldworker.

Great care needs to be taken by NGOs in distinguishing between truly representative organisations and those controlled by exploitative leaders. The group organised to confront national society may also decide to expel its fieldworkers, but for the reason that their objective has been achieved . Signs of tension between the fieldworkers and the indigenous group may be the perfectly healthy indication that the group is beginning to take over its own affairs. The NGO can respond in these cases by channelling funds directly through to the indigenous organisation.

An NGO which funds an indigenous organisation directly becomes increasingly concerned about the need for the group to have an independent income. Otherwise the NGO can become committed to long-term funding, greatly complicating eventual withdrawal. Very few indigenous organisations are completely independent financially, and the question of dependence on NGOs is an unresolved dilemma of self-management.

Withdrawing external agents from a project involves letting the people who have received training take fuller responsibility over decisions that were previously decided jointly with the fieldworkers. The ability of the indigenous project leaders to take greater responsibility will depend on the quality of the training they have received, the nature of the project and the complexity of the situation faced by the group.

10. Recommendations
i. Hand responsibility over early. Fieldworkers must not wait until indigenous project leaders are fully ready to take over the programme. Fieldworkers with high standards may feel the people never reach the right stage. It is always better to transfer responsibilities progressively from the start of the project, than to hand over abruptly.

ii. Let people learn from mistakes. Fieldworkers must not be inflexible over the details of project management, but be on hand when project leaders seek advice over mistakes. Indigenous people will only come for advice if relations with the fieldworker are not marred by criticism — be sparing with advice. Fieldworkers must always be supportive of project leaders but should also avoid being too quick to provide solutions when matters have gone wrong.

iii. Recognise your limits. Individual fieldworkers must constantly evaluate their professional input to the project, as the needs of indigenous organisations will vary as they develop. An anthropologist, for instance, might be essential to help the people organise and identify needs, but could later be replaced by other professionals such as doctors or agriculturalists.

iv. See tensions for what they are. Fieldworkers may be too closely involved to recognise a growing need for full independence. Outside evaluation may be necessary.

V. Success: The fieldworker as employee

Formally organised indigenous groups frequently need to engage professionals under contract for specific training projects. These fieldworkers will be directly accountable to the indigenous organisation and (ideally) will have little scope for imposing opinions and solutions on their indigenous employers. Although they will not face the difficulties of helping to design appropriate strategies for the group, their specific tasks will be complicated by the fact that their contracts are likely to be short-term, giving little time to adjust to conditions. They will depend heavily on briefings by other professionals who have worked in the same area. It is advisable to be quite clear what is expected of the fieldworker and whether this is consistent with his or her qualifications, with reasonable demands and with what the individual is prepared to contribute. Working hours need to be defined to avoid future problems (particularly with doctors) and if the fieldworker is living in a village setting the housing arrangements should permit times of privacy. The fieldworker will need to establish his or her credentials with the group early, and must earn sufficient respect to put across a personal point of view; otherwise there is a risk of being reduced to obeying the indigenous ruling body without the chance of suggesting alternatives or participating freely in discussion. To earn early respect, fieldworkers need to be aware that the people will judge them by their actions within a short time of arrival; too humble a start, in attempting to find one's feet, may be interpreted as weakness by a strong group. On the other hand, of course, an overly aggressive stance will not be tolerated. Fieldworkers should certainly not assume they know more than the people about their affairs, but neither should they give the impression that they know nothing. Working for indigenous organisations requires humility, confidence and competence.

To work for indigenous peoples and under their direction must always be the fieldworker's final objective. As the employee of an organisation formed to mediate with national society, the fieldworker has a clear position. It may be more difficult to keep this role in perspective in the shifting encampment of a group of nomadic foragers, and even more difficult when negotiating for land rights for a people who want no contact at all. The objective is always to work for indigenous peoples on terms which they decide. The risk of paternalism can never be averted, but it can be fought.

Background reading

Fieldworkers will find that two kinds of material are of particular use to them: general basic manuals for development workers, such as those listed in I below, and specific studies of the people and perhaps the nation state in which they are working. In II are listed some general works on the present situation of indigenous peoples, the relationship of anthropology and development etc., and some relevant periodicals. For a comprehensive ethnographic bibliography and a listing of NGOs concerned with indigenous affairs, see Goodland, below; for references on development which are of general rather than specifically indigenous application, see Oxfam's *Field Directors' Handbook.*

I. Technical Manuals

NGO representatives working with indigenous peoples will need technical manuals. We recommend in particular that this manual be used in conjunction with the following:

Roland Bunch (1982) *Two Ears of Corn — a guide to people-centred agricultural improvement,* World Neighbours, Oklahoma. Practical advice on all aspects of the subject, based on wide experience.

Murray Dickson (1983) *Where there is no Dentist.* The Hesperian Foundation, California. Companion to "Where there is no Doctor".

Oxfam (1985) *The Field Directors' Handbook,* ed. Brian Pratt and Jo Boyden, Oxford University Press. For reference on all subjects, particularly health and agriculture.

Oxfam (1987) *A Manual of Credit and Savings for the Poor of Developing Countries.*

David Werner (1977) *Where there is no Doctor.* The Hesperian Foundation, California. The basic manual for health care with minimal expenditure.

David Werner and Bill Bower (1982) *Helping Health Workers Learn.* The Hesperian Foundation, California. More than a health manual: gives instruction in invaluable techniques, such as drama and role play, of wide application in NGO projects with indigenous peoples.

II. Further Reading

M.G. Bicchieri (ed), *Hunters and Gatherers Today,* Holt, Rinehart and Winston, New York, 1972.

J. Burger, *Report from the Frontier — the state of the world's indigenous peoples,* Zed Press, London, 1987.

J. Galaty, D. Aronson, P. Salzman, *The Future of Pastoral Peoples,* IDRC, Ottawa, 1981.

W. Goldschmidt (ed), *The Uses of Anthropology,* Special Publication 11, American Anthropological Association, Washington D.C., 1979.

R. Goodland, *Tribal Peoples and Economic Development: Human Ecologic Considerations,* The World Bank, Washington D.C., 1982.

N.H.H. Graburn (ed), *Ethnic and Tourist Arts,* University of California Press, Berkeley, 1976.

R. Grillo and A. Rew (eds) *Social Anthropology and Development Policy,* Tavistock Publications. London and New York, 1985.

B.E. Harrell-Bond, *Imposing Aid: Emergency Assistance to Refugees,* Oxford University Press, Oxford, 1986.

G. Huizer and B. Mannheim (eds) *The Politics of Anthropology,* Mouton, The Hague, 1979.

Independent Commision on International Humanitarian Issues, *Indigenous Peoples — a global quest for justice,* Zed Press, London, 1987.

E. Leacock and R. Lee (eds), *Politics and History in Band Societies,* Cambridge University Press, Cambridge and Editions de la Maison des Sciences de l'Homme, Paris, 1982, paperback.

L. Mair, *Anthropology and Development,* Macmillan, London, 1984.

Minority Rights Group, *Reports* (see below).

N. Peterson and M. Langton (eds) *Aborigines, Land and Land Rights,* Australian Institute of Aboriginal Studies, Canberra, 1983.

The Reporter, Anti-Slavery Society (see below).

Survival International Review, Survival International (see below).

S. Sandford, *Management of Pastoral Development in the Third World,* Wiley, London and Chichester, 1983.

B. Whitaker, *The Fourth World: Victims of Group Oppression,* Sidgwick and Jackson, London, 1977.

B. Whitaker (ed.), *Minorities, A Question of Human Rights,* Pergamon Press, Oxford, 1984.

Organisations which support indigenous peoples

Some Names and Addresses of Organisations:

Anti-Slavery Society, 180 Brixton Road, London.

Cultural Survival, 11 Divinity Avenue, Cambridge, Mass. 02138, USA.

The Anthropological Resource Center, PO Box 15266, Washington D.C. 20003, USA.

Asociacion Interetnica de Desarollo de la Selva Peruana (AIDESEP), Avenida San Eugenio 981, Urbanisacion Santa Catalina, La Victoria, Lima, Peru.

Documentation and Information for Indigenous Affairs in the Amazon Region, 17 rue des Sources, 1205 Geneva, Switzerland.

Gesellschaft fur Bedrohte Volker (Society for Endangered Peoples), Postfach 159, 3400 Gottingen, Federal Republic of Germany.

International Work Group for Indigenous Affairs (IWGIA), Fiolstraede 10, DK-1171, Copenhagen K., Denmark.

Minority Rights Group, 29 Craven Street, London WC2.

Pastoral Development Network, Overseas Development Institute, Regents College, Inner Circle, Regents Park, London NW1.

Survival International for the rights of threatened tribal peoples, International Secretariat, 310 Edgware Road, London W2 1DY.